ML128.W7 S6
Women in American music : a bibliog

Y0-DNP-971

WOMEN IN AMERICAN MUSIC:

A Bibliography

by

JoAnn Skowronski

The Scarecrow Press, Inc.
Metuchen, N.J. & London
1978

Library of Congress Cataloging in Publication Data

Skowronski, JoAnn.
    Women in American music, a bibliography.

    Includes index.
    1. Women musicians, American--Bibliography.
I. Title.
ML128.W7S6   016.78'092'2   77-26611
ISBN 0-8108-1105-7

Copyright © 1978 by JoAnn Skowronski
Manufactured in the United States of America

This book is dedicated
to my husband
Ray
for his encouragement
and assistance

CONTENTS

Introduction	vii

BIBLIOGRAPHY

1	Betsy Ross's Revolutionary Times and the Early United States (1776-1834)	1
2	Coeducational Opportunities Begin for Women (1835-1868)	4
3	Suffragettes to World War II (1869-1938)	9
4	Rosie the Riveter and the Women's Liberation Movement (1939-1976)	43
5	General History	146
6	Bibliographies, Dictionaries, and Indexes	161
INDEX OF NAMES		167

INTRODUCTION

This bibliography presents information on literature which treats the subject of women in American music. Books on women's studies are of great interest since the women's liberation movement began and much research is being conducted in this area. This bibliography will be of special interest to the researcher examining the place of women in music from the birth of the United States until the present.

All areas of music are included in this bibliography, from religious to popular. Some foreign-born musicians, such as Jenny Lind, are included because they made significant contributions to the American musical scene.

The scope of this bibliography covers the years 1776-1976. This two-hundred-year survey of women in music starts with the official beginning of our nation since there is little material available on Colonial women in music. The two hundred years have been divided into four periods of time with significant events in the history of women being used as points of demarcation. Two additional divisions have been made: General history and Bibliographies, dictionaries, and indexes.

Entries, placed in the most appropriate section whenever the subject matter did not fit distinctly into one category, are arranged alphabetically by author within each section or by title if there was no author, editor, compiler or the like. All names which begin with "Mc" are filed as if they were spelled "Mac." The index at the end includes names which appear in both the entries and the annotations. The numbers which follow each name refer to the specific entries instead of pages.

This bibliography was compiled from many sources since there is no important reference work on this topic. Major periodical indexes such as the Readers' Guide and Music Index provided most of the periodical listings. Books

<u>in Print</u>, <u>Cumulative Book Index</u>, <u>National Union Catalog</u>, and bibliographies from music history books provided most of the book titles. Annotations were added whenever possible. Reference works such as biographical dictionaries were included when significant material was contained on the subject of women in music.

Several large university and public libraries in the Southern California area were utilized in this research.

1

BETSY ROSS'S REVOLUTIONARY TIMES AND THE EARLY UNITED STATES (1776-1834)

1 Clayton, Ellen Creathorne. Queens of Song. Freeport, N.Y.: Books for Libraries Press, 1972, c1865.
"Being memoirs of women of the most celebrated female vocalists who have performed on the lyric stage, from the earliest days of opera to the present time."

2 Cotton, John. Singing of Psalms; A Gospel Ordinance. London: Crowne In Popes-Head-Alley, 1647.
Chapter 8, "Wherebey [sic] Women May Sing as Well as Men," demonstrates Cotton's feelings that psalm singing was to be done by both sexes.

3 De Pauw, Linda Grant; Hunt, Conover; and Schneir, Miriam. Remember the Ladies: Women in America, 1750-1815. New York: Viking Press, 1976.
This study of the social conditions of women in early America indicates that fashionable and accomplished ladies were taught to sing and play a musical instrument in their fine arts education.

4 Johnson, Harold Earle. Musical Interludes in Boston, 1795-1830. New York: AMS Press, 1967, c1943.
A few women are mentioned in this thirty-five-year history of Boston music. One interesting subject discussed was marriage and the respectability required of women musicians.

5 Kmen, Henry. Music in New Orleans: The Formative Years, 1791-1841. Baton Rouge: Louisiana State University Press, 1966.
Minnie Hauk is one of the few women musicians mentioned in this early history of music in New Orleans.

6 Lawrence, Vera Brodsky. Music for Patriots, Politi-

cians, and Presidents; Harmonies and Discords of the First Hundred Years. New York: Macmillan, 1975.
   This large history of patriotic music, political ballads and songs has many facsimiles of music and pictures of this period. Few references are made to women. However, one area addressed to the subject of women is the discussion of "mother-songs," which were sentimental Civil War ballads about parting or loss of hope.

7 Leonard, Eugenie Andruss. The American Woman in Colonial and Revolutionary Times, 1565-1800; A Syllabus with Bibliography. Philadelphia: University of Pennsylvania Press, 1962.
   Includes some references to women musicians.

8 Mates, Julian. The American Musical Stage before 1800. New Brunswick, N.J.: Rutgers University Press, 1962.
   Opera and musical comedy are covered in this book along with references to many women who performed on the stage.

9 Pichierri, Louis. Music in New Hampshire, 1623-1800. New York: Columbia University Press, 1960.
   A history of music in this state as practiced before 1800. Women singers are discussed on pp. 207-208.

10 Rogers, F. "Some Prima Donnas of the Latter Eighteenth Century." Musical Quarterly 30:147-162, April 1944.
   Famous women singers who performed in America are included.

11 Sonneck, Oscar George Theodore. Early Concert-Life in America, 1731-1800. Wiesbaden: M. Sändig, 1969, c1907.
   Excellent source for the early period of American music with detailed references to the concert programs. The contributions of women as composers and performers are noted.

12 _____. Early Opera in America. New York: B. Blom, 1963, c1943.
   Covers American opera before the Revolutionary

War to about 1800. Many women singers are included in the discussion of early musical performance.

13 Stouramire, Albert. <u>Music of the Old South; Colony to Confederacy.</u> Rutherford, N.J.: Fairleigh Dickinson University Press, 1972.
A history of early music in the South. One of the centers of music culture (Richmond, Virginia) had prominent singers such as Jenny Lind and Adelina Patti appear there. Much information is given on the status music held in the lives of Southern women.

2
COEDUCATIONAL OPPORTUNITIES BEGIN FOR WOMEN (1835-1868)

14 Benêt, Laura. Enchanting Jenny Lind. New York: Dodd, Mead, 1939.
An extensive history of the concert life of Jenny Lind with details of her American tours in the 1850's.

15 Bulman, Joan. Jenny Lind; A Biography. London: James Barrie, 1956.
The life of Jenny Lind, the famous singer, with material about her popular American tours.

16 Cavanah, Frances. Jenny Lind's America. Philadelphia: Chilton Book Co., 1969.
"A biography of the 'Swedish Nightingale' whose vocal range and tone quality make her one of the leading opera stars of the mid-nineteenth century." She became a very popular singer in America.

17 Dunlap, Agnes Mary Robertson. The Swedish Nightingale: Jenny Lind. New York: Holt, Rinehart and Winston, 1964.
The biography of the singer Jenny Lind with details of her association with P. T. Barnum who brought her to America for concert tours.

18 "Elevating Influence of Music." Pennsylvania Freeman 9:4, February 19, 1852.
Jenny Lind, known as the Swedish Nightingale, received much publicity and acclaim during her concerts in the U.S.

19 "Emily Postism." Musical America 73:9, January 1, 1953.
Excerpts from True Politeness; A Handbook of Etiquette for Ladies published in 1847. Eight of its rules of grace pertain to music and are similar to the following admonition, "If nature has not given you a voice, do not attempt to sing."

20 "Extract from a Letter Describing Jenny Lind's First Appearance in Habana and the Sensation It Produced." North American Miscellany and Dollar Magazine 1: 143, February 15, 1851.

21 "Female Education." Musical Reporter 1:218-221, May 1841.
This article advocates including music in the curriculum for female education.

22 Ferris, George Titus. Great Singers: Faustina Bordoni to Henrietta Sontag. 2 vols. New York: D. Appleton, 1888.
Most of the singers discussed are women. Among them are Jenny Lind and Adelina Patti.

23 "The Fine Arts." Graham's American Monthly Magazine 43:332-334, April 1851.
Includes biographical information on various opera singers at this time.

24 Graves, A. J. Woman in America; Being an Examination into the Moral and Intellectual Condition of American Female Society. New York: Harper and Brothers, 1858, c1841.
Good overview of the place of women in society at the time. Some references made to the subjects offered to girls in school, including harp, guitar, and piano.

25 "A Hint to Musical Ladies." Musical Visitor 3:113, January 6, 1844.
The suggestion is that ladies avoid playing long compositions for visitors since it may tire them.

26 Humphrey, Laning. The Humor of Music and Other Oddities in the Art. Boston: Crescendo Publishing Co., 1971.
"They Didn't Need Women's Lib!" is a chapter dealing with the prominent place of women singers and the large salaries earned in concerts by Adelina Patti, Jenny Lind, and Mariette Alboni of earlier times.

27 Jackson, George Stuyvesant. Early Songs of Uncle Sam. Ann Arbor, Mich.: Gryphon Books, 1971, c1933.
Texts of popular songs printed about 1825-1850 are

covered in this work. Women are frequent subjects in these songs, which range from drinking songs to love songs.

28 "Letter to the Musical Times, London, January 1848." Music (AGO) 8:41, January 1974.
A letter from a chorister requesting that the discrimination against women's singing in church choirs be repealed. In early American church music the women sang tenor parts (the melody) but some church officials followed St. Paul's words, "Let the women be silent in church."

29 Levy, Lester. Flashes of Merriment; A Century of Humorous Songs in America, 1805-1905. Norman: University of Oklahoma Press, 1971.
This history of humorous songs contains a chapter on "Men and Women" which treats the comic aspects of romantic entanglements.

30 _____. Grace Notes in American History; Popular Sheet Music from 1820-1900. Norman: University of Oklahoma Press, 1967.
A history of the U.S. as depicted in popular songs of the time. It covers the mores of the people, such as the ridicule of "Mrs. Trollop's Quick Step." Information on the social position can be inferred from many of the lyrics which discuss women.

31 Maretzek, Max. Crotchets and Quavers; or, Revelations of an Opera Manager. New York: Da Capo Press, 1966, c1855.
Includes many of his experiences with temperamental female opera singers.

32 Maude, Mrs. Raymond. The Life of Jenny Lind. London: Cassell, 1926.
The biography of Jenny Lind who toured successfully in American cities, written by her daughter.

33 Moore, Frank. Songs and Ballads of the Southern People, 1861-1865. New York: B. Franklin, 1971, c1886.
Contains only lyrics and no music. Some of these are composed by women.

34 Moulton, Mrs. Charles. Sketch of Her Musical Career. New York: Baker & Goodwin, 1871.

35 "Musical Test of the Female Voice." Ladies Companion 4:56, December 1835.
The tone of the voice can be influenced greatly by temper according to this article.

36 "Rebecca Clarke, Violist and Composer." Strad 77:297, December 1966.
This Anglo-American woman had a successful career during the first half of the nineteenth century as a violist, teacher, and composer.

37 Ritter, Mrs. Frances Malone. Letters on Music to a Lady. Boston: Oliver Ditson, 1870.

38 Rush, [Dr.]. "Female Education." Boston Musical Gazette 1:149, January 4, 1839.
Dr. Rush's opinions on women's education in music. He felt it contributed to good health and would assist in better quality music in the churches.

39 Russell, Frank. Queen of Song; The Life of Henrietta Sontag. New York: Exposition Press, 1964.
The biography of this operatic soprano who sang in the U.S. during the 1850's. Included also are her opinions of America as revealed in her letters.

40 Scherman, Bernardine Kielty. Jenny Lind Sang Here. Boston: Houghton Mifflin, 1949.
A book for children stressing the American concerts of the soprano who was known as the Swedish Nightingale and was signed by P. T. Barnum to sing in America.

41 Shultz, Gladys Denny. Jenny Lind; The Swedish Nightingale. Philadelphia: J. B. Lippincott Co., 1962.
The career of this soprano is detailed with an emphasis on her concerts in the U.S. during the 1850's.

42 Simkins, Francis Butler, and Patton, James Welch. The Women of the Confederacy. Richmond, Va.: Garrett and Massie, 1936.
Chapter 14 on "Amusements and Social Diversions" describes how the ladies entertained during the Civil War. Singing and dancing utilizing local talent were the usual amusements.

43 Underwood, John Levi. The Women of the Confederacy. New York: Neale Pub. Co., 1906.

Detailed history of the part Southern women played in the Civil War. The major reference to their music is "The Southern Woman's Song"--five verses expressing the hope that their sewing would help their men in battle.

44 Wagenknecht, Edward Charles. *Jenny Lind.* Boston: Houghton Mifflin, 1931.
Includes details of Jenny Lind's singing in America.

45 Ware, William Porter, and Lockard, Thaddeus C. *The Lost Letters of Jenny Lind.* London: Victor Gollancz, 1966.
Some of these letters express Lind's feelings about the American concert tour under contract with P. T. Barnum.

46 "Young Ladies' Musical Education." *Musical Reporter* 1:22-26, January 1841.
The methods of music education of women need improvement at this time according to this article.

47 "Zeal of the Ladies." *Family Minstrel* 1:77, June 15, 1835.

3

SUFFRAGETTES TO WORLD WAR II (1869-1938)

48 Adams, M. "Foster-Mothers of Music." Woman Citizen n. s. 8:7-8, January 26, 1924.

49 Ahlers, Margaret Ann. "Value of Music Study to a Business Woman." Etude 52:56, January 1934.
    Ms. Ahlers feels that it is never too late to study music and that this type of hobby should refresh and enrich the business woman. A mature pupil, of course, progresses more quickly than a young one and this is to the business woman's advantage.

50 Albertson, Chris. Bessie. New York: Stein and Day, 1972.
    The biography of Bessie Smith who was a famous blues singer of the early twentieth century.

51 _____. "In Search of the Real Bessie Smith." Saturday Review 55:56, February 26, 1972.
    Albertson has carefully researched the life of this blues singer and has included information which had never before been included in other biographies.

52 Alda, Frances. Men, Women, and Tenors. Freeport, N.Y.: Books for Libraries Press, 1970, c1937.
    Ms. Alda's reminiscences of the years she spent as a performer at the New York Metropolitan Opera House.

53 Aldrich, Richard. Concert Life in New York, 1902-1923. New York: G. P. Putnam's Sons, 1941.

54 _____. Musical Discourse from the New York Times. London: Oxford University Press, 1929.
    Two chapters are devoted to women singers who gave concerts in New York: "Jenny Lind and Barnum" and "Adelina Patti in America."

55 Alvarez, Marguerite d'. <u>Forsaken Altars; Autobiography
of Marguerite d'Alvarez</u>. London: R. Hart-Davis,
1954.
   The operatic life of Alvarez who toured in America many times, once under contract to Oscar Hammerstein.

56 Alverson, Rosana Margaret Blake. <u>Sixty Years of California Songs</u>. Oakland, Calif.: M. B. Alverson, 1913.
   Ms. Alverson, a public singer and teacher of the late 1800's, gives an overview of music at that time. She includes much material on her students as well as other women musicians with whom she was acquainted.

57 Ames, Morgan. "First Lady of the Blues." <u>High Fidelity/Musical America</u> 20:86-87, October 1970.
   Bessie Smith the black blues singer is commemorated by Columbia Records in a projected series of ten albums containing all her recordings.

58 Anderton, Margaret. "It Is Woman Who Keeps Our Music A-going." <u>Musician</u> 33:11-21, August 1928.
   Elena Moneak was the founder and conductor of the Chicago Woman's Symphony Orchestra. Women's influence on the musical scene is discussed.

59 _____. "Motherhood and Music." <u>Musician</u> 31:17, May 1926.
   A discussion of a mother's influence on her children's attitude toward music.

60 _____. "What Women Are Doing for Music in America." <u>Musician</u> 34:33-34, January 1929.
   Mrs. William Arms Fisher of Boston has had a great influence on American music by encouraging quality performance.

61 "Antonia Brico Waves a Wand over a Dream Come True." <u>Newsweek</u> 5:22, March 2, 1935.
   The Women's Symphony of New York began its history with this performance led by Brico. Brico had conducted the orchestras of the Berlin Philharmonic, Detroit, and Buffalo.

62 "Antonia Brico's Triumph: First of Sex to Wield Baton

over N.Y. Philharmonic." Newsweek 12:21, August 1, 1938.

63 Arian, Edward. Bach, Beethoven, and Bureaucracy: The Case of the Philadelphia Orchestra. University: University of Alabama Press, 1971.
   The history of the Philadelphia Orchestra is explored. The Philadelphia Women's Committees played an important part in fund raising during the early 1900's.

64 Armsby, Leonora Wood. Musicians Talk. Freeport, New York: Books for Libraries Press, 1969, c1935.
   Mrs. Armsby records conversations and events associated with the San Mateo, California, concerts over a period of ten years.

65 Armstrong, William. "Girl Who Wants to Be a Singer." Ladies Home Journal 26:44, September 1909.

66 _____. The Romantic World of Music. Freeport, N.Y.: Books for Libraries Press, 1969, c1922.
   Singers from all over the world are discussed. Among them are several American women, including Lillian Nordica and Mary Garden.

67 Balliett, Whitney. "Bessie Smith Plain." New Yorker 49:128-129, February 24, 1973.
   A review of Chris Albertson's biography entitled Bessie.

68 "Band Mistress." Time 26:27, December 2, 1935.

69 Baral, Robert. Revue: A Nostalgic Reprise of the Great Broadway Period. New York: Fleet Pub. Corp., 1962.
   Broadway's productions of the past are often thought of in reference to the Ziegfeld Follies. Many women performers are included.

70 Barrell, Edgar A. "Notable Musical Women." Etude 47:805-806, 897, November-December 1929; 48:12, 92, 164, 246, January-April 1930.
   Brief biographical information on women musicians, chiefly contemporary, from all over the world.

71 Barrientos, M. "Prima-Donna's Story." Forum 62: 197-205, August 1919.

72 Bauer, E. F. "Mrs. Coolidge, Music Philanthropist." Woman Citizen n. s. 10:12, November 1925.

73 Beach, Amy Marcy. "Amer. Sym.: H. H. A. Beach Cto. Performed in Hempstead, N. Y." High Fidelity/Musical America 26:29-30, July 1976.
    Mrs. H. H. A. Beach's "Piano Concerto in C Sharp Minor" was first performed in 1900 by the Boston Symphony and was revived at this performance at Calderone Hall in Hempstead.

74 "Bessie's Blues." Time 30:38, November 22, 1937.
    Bessie Smith the blues singer is discussed.

75 Blesh, Rudi, and Janis, Harriet. They All Played Ragtime. Rev. ed. New York: Oak Publications, 1966.
    Ragtime is treated as a separate aspect of jazz in this book. Some women were involved in ragtime such as May Irwin and Kate Ross.

76 Bloom, Clifford. "Excellent Program of Compositions by American Women." Etude 45:184, March 1927.
    The composers include Mrs. H. H. A. Beach, Helen Ware, Lilly Strickland, and thirteen others.

77 Brackett, Anna Callender. Woman and the Higher Education. New York: Harper & Brothers, 1893.
    Music was generally part of the liberal education women received in early American colleges.

78 Brower, Edith. "Is the Musical Idea Masculine?" Atlantic Monthly 73:332-339, March 1894.
    An essay on the problems women composers face in trying to have their creative work taken seriously.

79 Brower, Harriette. "Girl and Her Music in the Small Town." Woman's Home Companion 38:37, October 1911.

80 _____. "How Margarete Dessoff Overcame an Age-Old Tradition." Musician 32:13, July 1927.
    Dessoff overcame the prejudice against women conductors and became a guest conductor of the Schola Cantorum in New York. She relates how she began conducting choral groups and managed to switch to conducting orchestras.

81 _____. "Wake Up, Miss America." Etude 39:715-716, November 1921.
An address to girls who are "passionately fond of music" but have difficulty becoming good musicians.

82 Brown, Mrs. P. H. "One and Only Band." St. Nicholas 54:24, November 1926.

83 Burr, H. H. "American Women-Musicians." Cosmopolitan 31:357-364, August 1901.

84 "Cantankerous Queens of the Opera." Literary Digest 98:27, July 7, 1928.
Operatic stars, especially the ladies, are often known for their ill temperament. Details of the most vivid scenes are recalled in this article.

85 "Cape Cod's Distinguished School of the Arts Founded by Martha Atwood Baker." Musician 45:88, May 1940.
Martha A. Baker's dream was to bring cultural advantages to Cape Cod. This became a reality when she established the Cape Cod Institute of Music.

86 Charters, Samuel Barclay. The Bluesmen; The Story and the Music of the Men Who Made the Blues. New York: Oak Publications, 1967.
Information about women who were associated with well-known singers is included, such as Bertha Lee's asssociation with Charley Patton. There is extensive discussion of song lyrics which to a large degree revolve around the women in the bluesmen's lives.

87 _____. The Country Blues. London: Jazz Book Club, 1961, c1959.
Few women are mentioned in this book of blues; Bessie Smith is one of the most predominant ones.

88 _____ and Kunstadt, Leonard. Jazz; A History of the New York Scene. Garden City, N.Y.: Doubleday, 1962.
The book focuses on the history of jazz in New York, from brass bands through Dixieland. Prominent jazz women such as Bessie Smith and Ella Fitzgerald performed in New York and are included in the discussion.

89 Clark, N. M. "Carrie Jacobs-Bond Has Written Her Life into Her Songs." American Magazine 97:18-20, January 1924.

90 Colson, Percy. Melba; An Unconventional Biography. London: Grayson & Grayson, 1932.
Biography of the Australian soprano Nellie Melba who performed in America as well as many other countries.

91 Comfort, Annabel. "Marjorie Lawrence and Achievement!" Etude 56:593-594, September 1938.
An interview with Lawrence relating her success in Paris and New York. She answers personal questions about her schedule as an opera star and gives advice to those aspiring to an operatic career.

92 Cone, John Frederick. Oscar Hammerstein's Manhattan Opera Company. Norman: University of Oklahoma Press, 1966.
The brief history of New York's Manhattan Opera Company under Hammerstein's direction. Performers such as Mary Garden are discussed.

93 Confessions of a Prima Donna. New York: Frederick A. Stokes, 1924.

94 Cooke, James Francis. Great Men and Famous Musicians on the Art of Music; Educational Conferences with Representative Men and Women. Philadelphia: Theodore Presser Co., 1925.

95 _____. Great Singers on the Art of Singing: Educational Conferences with Foremost Artists. Philadelphia: Theodore Presser Co., 1921.
"A series of personal study talks with the most renowned opera, concert and oratorio singers of the time, especially planned for voice students."

96 Cooper, Arthur. "Blue Empress: Bessie." Newsweek 81:92, January 22, 1973.
A review of Chris Albertson's book Bessie which deals with the life of the Negro blues singer Bessie Smith.

97 Corbin, John. "Geraldine Farrar's Advice to Aspiring Singers." Good Housekeeping 53:12-19, July 1911.

98 Cushing, Mary Finch Watkins. Behind the Scenes at the Opera; Intimate Revelations of Backstage Musical Life and Work. New York: Frederick A. Stokes Co., 1925.
　　Principally concerned with opera singers.

99 _____. "Operatic Ladies in Retirement." Opera News 18:6, March 8, 1954.
　　Information about Grete Stueckgold, one of the youngest singers to excel in opera. She retired from the Metropolitan Opera House in 1934 and resided in New York.

100 _____. The Rainbow Bridge. New York: Putnam, 1954.
　　Ms. Cushing's story of her life as the traveling companion of the opera star Olive Fremstad. Many of Fremstad's performances were in America.

101 Dance, Stanley. "The Empress Still Reigns." Saturday Review 53:41, August 29, 1970.
　　Bessie Smith's blues recordings are being combined and released in five sets of two records each by Columbia Records.

102 Daughtry, Willia Estelle. "Sissieretta Jones: A Study of the Negro's Contribution to Nineteenth Century American Concert and Theatrical Life." Ph.D. dissertation, Syracuse University, 1968.
　　A study of Jones who was a concert and theater singer in early America. Her career is contrasted with that of other Negro performers at that time.

103 Davis, M. "Can Women Write Songs?" Pictorial Review 37:10, November 1935.

104 Dean, F. "Beauty on the Operatic Stage." Munsey 29:97-106, April 1903.

105 Debrant, Cyr. "Composers and Their Mothers." Etude 58:297-298, May 1940.
　　The contributions that mothers of many famous men have made for their children's musical education is noted. Among the musicians discussed are the Americans Edward MacDowell and Ethelbert Nevin.

106 De Koven, Anna Farwell. A Musician and His Wife.

New York: Harper & Brothers, 1926.
Mrs. De Koven's autobiography.

107 Drummond, Robert Rutherford. <u>Early German Music in Philadelphia</u>. New York: Da Capo, 1970, c1910.
Women are mentioned in relation to concert music, chiefly as performers.

108 Eaton, Quaintance. <u>The Boston Opera Company</u>. New York: Appleton-Century, 1965.
The early history of the Boston Opera Company contains a significant number of famous women singers, such as Mary Garden and Lillian Nordica.

109 _____. "Ladies on the Loose-Itinerant Prima Donnas Aren't What They Used to Be." <u>Opera News</u> 30: 32-34, October 23, 1965.
Opera stars such as Minnie Hauk and Clara Louise Kellogg used to travel a great deal on the American "road" to give performances, especially during the last half of the nineteenth century.

110 Edwards, E. Harlow. "Shall I Study with a Man or a Woman?" <u>Etude</u> 50:756a, October 1932.

111 Erb, J. Lawrence. "Utilizing Women's Voices." <u>Etude</u> 46:54, January 1928.
There is often a lack of men's voices in church choirs. Mr. Erb suggests emphasizing the women's choir as a successful solution to this problem, and includes a list of anthems which are suitable for female voices.

112 "Farmers' Opera; All Rural Production of The Bohemian Girl, Ames, Iowa." <u>Time</u> 26:39, July 1, 1935.
An opera production by 4-H club members and other rural Iowans was the fifteen-year dream of the state 4-H club leader, Josephine Bakke.

113 Farrar, Geraldine. <u>The Autobiography of Geraldine Farrar: Such Sweet Compulsion</u>. New York: Da Capo Press, 1970, c1939.
An American singer who became very popular.

114 _____. "Girl Who Wants to Sing." <u>Ladies Home Journal</u> 31:29, October 1914.

115 _____. "What Must I Go Through to Become a Prima Donna?" Etude 38:367-368, June 1920.
An interview with the distinguished American singer Geraldine Farrar about the problems of becoming a great operatic singer.

116 Ffrench, Florence. Music and Musicians in Chicago; The City's Leading Artists, Organizations and Art Buildings, Progress and Development. Chicago: F. French, 1899.
Many sections in this history are by and about women of Chicago. A good history of music in this city is given, covering 1836-1899. Women played an extensive role in the Chicago music scene according to this work.

117 Finck, Henry Theophilus. "Modern Improvements in Prima Donnas." Musician 14:20-21, January 1909.

118 _____. My Adventures in the Golden Age of Music. New York: Da Capo Press, 1971, c1926.
Many prominent women singers from America as well as other parts of the world are discussed in Part V: "The Golden Age in Musical New York--and After."

119 _____. "Women in Music To-day." Nation 106:664, June 1, 1918.
An article which indicates that there are many women musicians in all parts of the world who are achieving success in areas of music other than singing.

120 Fischer, D. B. "The Story of New Orlean's Rise As a Music Center." Musical America 19:3-5, March 14, 1914.
Traces the history of concert music in New Orleans with a large portion of the material devoted to the contributions of the women of the city in pressing for increased musical activities.

121 Fletcher, Tom. 100 Years of the Negro in Show Business; The Tom Fletcher Story. New York: Burdge, 1954.
This account of a century of black performers was written by a man who was active in this field. Fletcher tells of many lesser-known performers in show business of which many were women.

122 Ford, F. G. "Famous Prima Donnas of Old." New England Magazine n.s. 32:259-269, May 1905.

123 Foster, O. H. "Mother as a Music Teacher." Ladies Home Journal 21:20, September 1904.

124 Frame, Florence K. "Women Also Conduct Orchestras." Music Journal 15:25, February 1957.
   Antonia Brico in 1938 was the first woman to conduct the New York Philharmonic. However, this was not her first appearance on the podium. She had conducted the Detroit and the New York Women's Symphony earlier.

125 Franklin, C. J. "How Miss Watson Boosted Her Bank Account." Etude 51:574, September 1933.
   An article which demonstrates a good method of gaining new pupils by proper salesmanship. By selling them the Etude, parents and children will be inspired to study music seriously.

126 Freer, E. E. "Woes of a Woman Composer." Overland Monthly n.s. 82:458, October 1924.

127 "From Wonderchild to Diva." Etude 42:667-668, October 1924.
   An interview with opera star Madame Marcella Sembrich. Although born in Poland, she studied and sang extensively in Europe and the U.S. She later became a faculty member at the Curtis Institute of Music.

128 "Fuller Sisters." Harper's Weekly 58:25, January 31, 1914.

129 Garden, Mary. "American Girl and Music." Good Housekeeping 56:168-174, February 1913.

130 _____ and Biancolli, Louis. Mary Garden's Story. New York: Simon and Schuster, 1951.
   The autobiography of Mary Garden, the opera singer from Aberdeen who sang and lectured in the U.S.

131 Gatti-Casazza, Guilo. "Chances of the American Girl in Opera." Etude 41:151, March 1923.
   Mr. Gatti-Casazza, general director of the Metropolitan Opera Company, feels that there is ample

opportunity in the field of opera for the truly talented singer who is well schooled in the old music of classic operas.

132 _____. "My Thirty Years in Opera." Ladies Home Journal 13:32, March; 44, April; 40, May; 44, June 1926.

133 Gaul, H. B. "Woman in Music." Musician 21:143, March 1916.

134 Gaume, Mary Matilda. "Ruth Crawford Seeger: Her Life and Works." Ph.D. dissertation, Indiana University, 1973.
The music and life of this American composer of the first half of the twentieth century is examined. The influence of American folk songs on her works is scrutinized and personal interviews with her friends and relatives are included.

135 Gilhagen, E. "Eve Gets a Thrill." Independent Woman 16:65, March 1937.

136 _____. "Up the Musical Scale." Independent Woman 17:83-84, March 1938.
Discussion of women as musicians.

137 Gilman, Lawrence. Phases of Modern Music. Freeport, N.Y.: Books for Libraries Press, 1968, c1904.
The subject of "Women and Modern Music" is treated in this book of essays on pp. 93-101. Gilman gives his theories as to why there have been few successful women composers.

138 Gipson, Richard M. The Life of Emma Thursby, 1845-1931. New York: New York Historical Society, 1940.
This soprano from New York was a prominent voice teacher.

139 Glackens, Ira. Yankee Diva; Lillian Nordica and the Golden Days of Opera. New York: Coleridge Press, 1963.
The biography of this nineteenth-century soprano from Maine.

140 Goldberg, Isaac. Tin Pan Alley; A Chronicle of the American Popular Music Racket. New York: John

Day Co., 1930.
A story of popular music in America which includes few references to women's contributions. Some scattered references to women are found, such as Maude Nugent who sang "Sweet Rosie O'Grady."

141 Grau, R. "Strange Public Aversion to Contraltos As Compared with the Sopranos of Great Fame." Musician 21:694, November 1916.

142 Hackett, K. "Economic Value of Music to Women." Musician 18:13, January 1913.

143 Hadden, J. Cuthbert. "Music and Matrimony." Cornhill Magazine 79:479-506, April 1899.
Hadden's article examines the problems male musicians face by getting married.

144 _____. "Prima Donna." Cornhill Magazine 71:73-85, January 1895.
An essay on the capriciousness of opera singers (both men and women) of the past with examples of their behavior.

145 Hadlock, Richard. Jazz Masters of the Twenties. New York: Macmillan Co., 1965.
One of the nine chapters is devoted to Bessie Smith, the only woman who had a significant influence on jazz during the 1920's according to this work.

146 Hageman, Richard. "Shall the Young Woman Choose Music As a Profession?" Musician 30:9-10, March 1925.
Hageman emphasized that there is a lot of preparation necessary to become a teacher or performer and that a woman should consider her priorities carefully before making this decision.

147 Hallock, M. "Women's Music Clubs." Musician 16:581, September 1911.

148 Hammerstein, Oscar. "Future for the American Prima Donna." Delineator 73:564, April 1909.

149 Hare, Maud Cuney. Negro Musicians and Their Music. New York: Da Capo Press, 1974, c1936.
Many lesser-known Negro women musicians are discussed in the chapter on "Musical Pioneers."

150 Hartt, R. L. "Beth Tries to Understand Music." Woman's Home Companion 40:30, January 1913.

151 Hauk, Minnie. Memoirs of a Singer. London: A. M. Philpot, 1925.
Autobiographical work of this American singer.

152 Hetherington, John. Melba; A Biography. New York: Farrar, Straus & Giroux, 1967.
Nellie Melba was an Australian soprano who toured in America around the 1900's.

153 Heylbut, Rose, and Gerber, Aimé. Backstage at the Opera. New York: Thomas Y. Crowell, 1937.
Discussion of opera at the Metropolitan Opera House in New York around the 1900's.

154 Hipsher, Edward Ellsworth. "American Girl's Chance in Opera." Etude 47:801-802, November 1929.
An interview with the American soprano Rosa Ponselle. She believes that the opportunities in opera are excellent for the truly talented girl who has had proper training.

155 _____. American Opera and Its Composers. Philadelphia: Theodore Presser Co., 1927.
Includes information on a few American women who were important in the history of opera such as Mary Carr Moore (a composer) and Harriet Ware (a composer and pianist).

156 History of Music Project. Celebrities in El Dorado, 1850-1906. San Francisco: Work Projects Administration, 1940.
Short biographies of 111 musicians who performed in the San Francisco area during this time, many of whom were American women singers.

157 _____. Fifty Local Prodigies. San Francisco: Work Projects Administration, 1940.
All of these young people were from the San Francisco vicinity and had shown musical talent. Many were girls.

158 _____. Music of the Gold Rush Era. San Francisco: Work Projects Administration, 1939.
Some well-known prima donnas were brought in to

sing in the San Francisco operas of this time. In addition, a few local women became known for their vocal abilities.

159 Homer, L. "Opera Training and the American Girl." Good Housekeeping 54:616-622, May 1912.

160 Hopkins, Jerome. "Music and Snobs"; or, a Few Funny Facts Regarding the Disabilities of Music in America. New York: R. A. Saalfield, 1888.
   Mr. Hopkins decries some of the customs and laws regarding music at the time, such as the little girl who was arrested for singing in a New York theatre.

161 "How Women Are Swindled in Music." Ladies Home Journal 26:8, March 1909.

162 Howard, John Tasker. Our Contemporary Composers: American Music in the Twentieth Century. New York: Thomas Y. Crowell Co., 1941.
   Howard writes chiefly of composers of the 1930's and includes a section on "Women Composers," pp. 72-74. Information about the works of six women is given.

163 Howard, Kathleen. Confessions of an Opera Singer. New York: A. A. Knopf, 1918.
   This contralto, actress, and writer from Canada spent part of her career working in California.

164 Hughes, E. "American Singers in European Opera-Houses." World To-day 17:824-832, August 1909.

165 Hughes, Rupert. "Music in America--The Women Composers." Godey's Magazine 132:30-40, January 1896.

166 _____. "Women Composers." Century Magazine 55:768-769, March 1898.
   A discussion of the works of some women composers including the Americans Mrs. H. H. A. Beach, Margaret Ruthven Lang, and Clara A. Korn.

167 Huneker, J. G. "Feminism in Modern Music." Harper's Bazaar 39:691-694, August 1905.

168 _____. "Girl Who Plays Chopin." Harper's Bazaar 33:466-468, June 23, 1900.

169 Irons, M. E. 'When Mother Sings: Mothersingers." Education 56:559-563, May 1936.

170 "Is Woman a Failure As a Creative Musician?" Current Opinion 72:776-777, June 1922.
J. Swinburne, an English music critic, feels that women have composed no music of value. D. C. Parker adds that women have not excelled in any area of music, even as music critics.

171 Jeritza, Maria. "The Business of Being a Prima Donna." Saturday Evening Post 196:20-21, February 2, 1924.
This opera singer tells of the problems she encountered in her debut at the New York Metropolitan Opera. In addition, she outlines the tedious working schedule of an operatic performer.

172 _____. Sunlight and Song; A Singer's Life. New York: Appleton, 1924.
Jeritza is a dramatic soprano who gave many concerts in the U. S. where she married and settled down.

173 Johnson, Frances Hall. Musical Memories of Hartford. New York: AMS Press, 1970, c1931.
Chapter 14, entitled "Mrs. Charles Dudley Warner," tells how she became a leader in the musical life of the community.

174 "Juliette Crosby Adams." Musician 21:199-200, April 1916.
Ms. Adams was a music teacher.

175 Kelley, Mrs. Edgar Stillman. "Blessed Is the Musical Woman." Etude 47:806, November 1929.
As president of the National Federation of Music Clubs in 1929, Mrs. Kelley writes that she finds no drudgery in the life of a musician and feels the study of music is a noble pursuit.

176 Kellogg, Clara Louise. Memoirs of an American Prima Donna. New York: G. P. Putnam's Sons, 1913.
Autobiography of this opera singer's life.

177 Kempf, Paul. "Think for Yourself, Express Yourself, Miss Farrar Advises Students." Musician 29:11, October 1924.

Geraldine Farrar, the famous opera singer, discourages young singers from following opera traditions. She encourages American girls to be creative in their singing and interpretations.

178 Kennedy, J. B. "Ladies of the Air Waves." Collier's 90:14, July 9, 1932.

179 Kobbé, Gustav. Opera Singers; A Pictorial Souvenir, with Biographies of Some of the Most Famous Singers of the Day. Boston: Oliver Ditson Co., 1904.

180 Krebs, T. L. "Women As Musicians." Sewanee Review 2:76-87, November 1893.
An examination of the influence women have had in music history through the ages and includes some Americans of the 1890's.

181 Ladd, George Trumbull. Why Women Cannot Compose Music. New Haven, Conn.: Yale Publication Association, 1917.

182 Lahee, Henry Charles. The Grand Opera Singers of To-day; An Account of the Leading Operatic Stars Who Have Sung During Recent Years, Together with a Sketch of the Chief Operatic Enterprises. Boston: L. C. Page, 1912.
"Some accounts of leading singers who were popular in America."

183 Larkin, Margaret. "Ella May's Songs." Nation 129: 382-383, October 9, 1929.
Ella Mae Wiggins composed "Song Ballets" for the union meetings of the Southern Textile Workers. The article includes some of the ballad lyrics she composed.

184 Lawton, Mary. Schumann-Heink, the Last of the Titans. New ed. New York: Macmillan, 1929.
A biography of the great Austrain singer who sang in American operas. Her personal experiences in the United States are explored.

185 Lehmann, Lilli. My Path Through Life. New York: G. P. Putnam's Sons, 1914.
German singer who performed in America.

186 Lehmann, Lotte. Midway in My Song; The Autobiography of Lotte Lehmann. Indianapolis: Bobbs-Merrill Co., 1938.
   Lotte Lehmann's story of her life as a singer from Germany with details of her concert tours in America.

187 _____. My Many Lives. New York: Boosey & Hawkes, 1948.
   Lotte Lehmann writes about the many characters she has portrayed in her operatic career. She performed in America after she became popular in Europe.

188 Le Massena, Clarence Edward. Galli-Curci's Life of Song. New York: Paebar Co., 1945.
   The biography of Amelita Galli-Curci. This famous opera singer was from Europe but sang in the U.S. and later settled here.

189 Leonard, Florence. "Fundamental Art Secrets in Piano Playing." Etude 47:803, November 1929.
   An interview with the German pianist Elly Ney who made her home in Chicago. She noted that the fundamentals of music are the same all over the world. Most of her emphasis was on the tonal quality of music.

190 Lonergan, Elizabeth. "American Women Musicians." Strand 42:654-655, December 1911.

191 McCall, A. B. "Girl's Education in Music." Woman's Home Companion 39:27, March 1912.

192 McCormack, Lily Foley. I Hear You Calling Me. Milwaukee: Bruce Pub. Co., 1949.
   Biography of this Irish singer which included information on her American concerts.

193 MacDowell, Mrs. Edward. "Woman's Opportunity in Music." Etude 47:798, November 1929.
   Opportunities for a career as a concert artist were few, but opportunities for a profession as a music teacher were excellent in 1929.

194 Macleod, Joseph. The Sisters d'Aranyi. London: Allen and Unwin, 1969.
   A biography of these musical sisters from Hungary: Adila, Hortense Emilia, and Jelly. One chapter covers "Myra Hess and America."

195 McRae, B. "The Ma Rainey and Bessie Smith Accompaniments." Jazz Journal 14:6-8, March 1961.
   Treats the subjects of accompaniments used by these two women blues singers.

196 Majors, M. A. Noted Negro Women. Chicago: Donahue and Henneberry, 1893.
   Among the singers is Sissieretta Jones who was very active in the American theater.

197 Mapleson, James Henry. The Mapleson Memoirs; The Career of an Operatic Impresario, 1858-1888. New York: Appleton-Century, 1966.
   Mapleson's memoirs are considered an excellent sourcebook of operatic history of England and America. Among his reminiscences are many women with whom he worked, such as Minnie Hauk and Clara Louise Kellogg.

198 Maretzek, Max. Revelations of an Opera Manager in 19th-Century America. Crotchets and Quavers & Sharps and Flats. New York: Dover Publications, 1968.
   Crotchets and Quavers was originally published in 1855 and Sharps and Flats in 1890. Maretzek was an opera manager who revealed his experiences with opera singers during the 1800's.

199 "Marian Cox Tells Why Women Love Music." Current Opinion 68:349-350, March 1920.
   Ms. Cox contrasts the varying degrees of receptiveness that men and women have for music. Her essay includes some possible biological reasons for these differences.

200 Marks, Edward Bennet. They All Sang, from Tony Pastor to Rudy Valée. New York: Viking Press, 1934.
   A discussion of the popular singers of New York around 1900. Women were the subjects of many of these songs, and there were many female singers and dancers at this time as well.

201 Marsh, J. B. T. The Story of the Jubilee Singers; With Their Songs. Rev. ed. New York: Negro Universities Press, 1969, c1881.
   Personal histories of these men and women are

included along with a chronicle of their tours around the world.

202 Marsh, Robert Charles. The Cleveland Orchestra. Cleveland: World Pub. Co., 1967.
 Adella Prentiss Hughes was a central figure in the Cleveland Orchestra's establishment. In 1898 she became an impresario. Under her direction the programs and financial support increased significantly.

203 Martens, Frederick Herman. The Art of the Prima Donna and Concert Singer. New York: D. Appleton and Co., 1923.
 "Interviews with Farrar, Jeritza, Galli-Curci, and others, who tell 'in a direct, informal manner ... what they did to achieve their success on the operatic and concert stage.'"--Introduction.

204 Mason, Daniel Gregory. Tune In, America! A Study of Our Coming Musical Independence. Freeport, N.Y.: Books for Libraries Press, 1969, c1931.
 "Includes lists of American works played by leading orchestras during 1925/26-1929/30 and a list of chamber music works by American composers."

205 May, E. C. "Women on the Air." Pictorial Review 36:22, October 1934.

206 Maynard, Clarke. "Lillian Baldwin and the Cleveland Story." Etude 72:13, December 1954.
 Cleveland schools have had an ambitious musical education program since 1929 under the leadership of Lillian Baldwin. Details of the music appreciation projects are given.

207 Melba, Nellie. "Girl with a Voice; Why She Should Be Careful in Her Decision to Study Abroad." Ladies Home Journal 26:31, April 1909.

208 _____. Melodies and Memories. Freeport, N.Y.: Books for Libraries Press, 1970, c1926.
 The autobiography of this Australian opera singer along with information about her concert experiences in the U.S.

209 _____. "Two Favorite Songs and How I Sing Them." Woman's Home Companion 42:6, September 1915.

210 Mellish, Mary Flannery. *Sometimes I Reminisce; Autobiography.* New York: G. P. Putnam's Sons, 1941.

211 Meltzer, C. H. "Mary Garden and *Louise*." *Review* 2:162-164, February 14, 1920.
   Review of Mary Garden's opera performance in the U.S.

212 "Men and Women As Organists." *Musician* 33:31, August 1928.
   Sex discrimination is examined in relation to organist's positions. Women are free to take small jobs in the music field that are available. Suitable salaries for women would be inadequate for men according to this article.

213 Merington, M. "Heroines of the Wagnerian Libretti." *Harper's Bazaar* 33:140-141, February 17, 1900.

214 Merz, Karl. *Music and Culture; Comprising a Number of Lectures and Essays.* Philadelphia: T. Presser, 1890.
   Chapter 13, "Women in Music," gives Merz's philosophy of music education as a Christian art for women.

215 Meyer, Annie. *Woman's Work in America.* New York: H. Holt and Co., 1891.
   The place of music is briefly touched upon in regard to education. More emphasis is on the place of women in professions as law, medicine, and journalism.

216 Milinowski, Marta. *Teresa Carreño.* Caracas: Ediciones Edime, 1953.
   This famous pianist, composer, and singer from Carácas gave her first concert at age eight in New York where she later settled down.

217 Miller, M. "What Music May Mean to the Adolescent Girl." *Musician* 23:96, February 1918.

218 "Miss Bessie's Blues." *Time* 96:40, August 3, 1970.
   Bessie Smith is the blues singer whose style is discussed.

219 Moore, Grace. *You're Only Human Once.* New York: Doubleday, 1944.

An American soprano's autobiography of her career at the Metropolitan Opera and other opera houses of the U.S. and Europe.

220 More, D. "Her Voice--and Her Soul: Should Your Daughter Go Alone to the City to Study?" Good Housekeeping 57:630-636, November 1913.

221 Murphy, Agnes G. Melba. London: Chatto and Windus, 1909.
The story of Nellie Melba, an opera singer from Australia who toured in the United States.

222 "Music Student; Small-Town Girl Who Came to New York to Seek Musical Fame." Scribner's Magazine 98:307-310, November 1935.
A story which is relevant to the experiences of many young musicians in their attempt to launch a successful career.

223 "Music Teaching As a Livelihood for Women in the United States." Musician 15:448, July 1910.

224 Mussulman, Joseph A. Music in the Cultured Generation; A Social History of Music in America, 1870-1900. Evanston, Ill.: Northwestern University Press, 1971.
Chapter 8, "Opera for America," discusses some of the foremost women singers who performed in American operas before 1900.

225 National Portrait Gallery. A Glimmer of Their Own Beauty: Black Sounds of the Twenties. Washington, D.C.: Smithsonian Institution, 1971.
Much of this short book is devoted to three black women in jazz: Gertrude "Ma" Rainey, Bessie Smith, and Lil Hardin Armstrong.

226 Nearing, Scott, and Nearing, Nellis M. S. Woman and Social Progress; A Discussion of the Biologic, Domestic, Industrial and Social Possibilities of American Women. New York: Macmillan Co., 1912.
In the area of education, the authors felt there was "no reason why she should not adopt a profession and follow it through life...." The example of singer Madame Gadski was given. However, in general, the education of women consisted of basic writing and math, and sometimes music and dancing. In the

college curriculum, almost equal opportunity was offered to both sexes.

227 Nordica, Lillian. *Lillian Nordica's Hints to Singers.* New York: E. P. Dutton, 1923.

228 _____. "Prima Donna and Her Task." *Harper's Weekly* 49:1676, November 18, 1905.

229 Northcutt, John Orlando. *Symphony: The Story of the Los Angeles Philharmonic Orchestra.* Los Angeles: Southern California Symphony Association, 1963.
The Los Angeles Philharmonic has had forty-seven women on its roster from its beginnings in 1919 until 1963. In addition, the Los Angeles Women's Symphony Orchestra began in 1893 and was one of the ancestors of the Los Angeles Philharmonic.

230 Oliver, Paul. *Aspects of the Blues Tradition.* New York: Oak Publications, 1970.
A history and analysis of blues with a few references to women in the field such as the singer Bessie Smith.

231 _____. *Bessie Smith.* New York: Barnes, 1961, c1959.

232 _____. *Blues Fell This Morning; The Meaning of the Blues.* New York: Horizon Press, 1961.
An examination of blues in America which includes famous black women singers such as Ma Rainey.

233 _____. "Ma Rainey Was Here." *Jazz Monthly* 11:21-23, March 1965.

234 _____. *Screening the Blues: Aspects of the Blues Tradition.* London: Cassell, 1968.
Women blues singers such as Bessie Smith and St. Louis Bessie (Bessie Mae Smith) are analyzed in this work.

235 _____. *The Story of the Blues.* Philadelphia: Chilton Book Co., 1969.
A few black women blues singers are included; Bessie Smith is one of the most prominent women included, but lesser-known women are noted as well.

236 Olsson, Bengt. Memphis Blues and Jug Bands. London: Studio Vista, 1970.
Traces the background of the jug bands and the blues musicians of Memphis including the women Hattie Hart and Laura Duke.

237 "Orchestral Women." Scientific American 73:327, November 23, 1895.
An argument against admitting women to orchestras because of their lack of physical stamina needed for long hours of rehearsal and performance.

238 "Our Front-Rank Feminine Songbirds." Literary Digest 88:26-27, February 27, 1926.
Critiques of the vocal capabilities of women who were singing at the Metropolitan Opera in 1926, including Maria Jeritza, Rosa Ponselle, and Florence Easton.

239 "Pages Selected from a Girl's Diary." Musician 14:451, October 1909.
Concerns singing and voice culture.

240 Panassié, Hughes. Hot Jazz; The Guide to Swing Music. Rev. ed. Westport, Conn.: Negro Universities Press, 1970, c1936.
References are found to the most prominent women in jazz, but few details are given.

241 Panser, R. M. "Stepdaughters of Orpheus." Independent Woman 15:39, February 1936.
Women as musicians are discussed.

242 Parker, Henry Taylor. Eighth Notes: Voices and Figures of Music and the Dance. Freeport, N.Y.: Books for Libraries Press, 1968, c1922.
Most of this book was drawn from the Boston Evening Transcript. Much discussion about women who toured in the U.S. is included.

243 Patten, M. "Singing State: Iowa!" Recreation 31:484-485, November 1937.
"Mammoth festival at Tenth Annual 4-H Girls' Club Convention at Iowa State College."

244 Peltz, Mary Ellis Opdycke. Spotlights on the Stars; Intimate Sketches of Metropolitan Opera Personalities.

New York: Metropolitan Opera Guild, 1943.

245 Pert, Yvonne. "Women in Music; An English Writer's Opinion of Some Present Day Composers." Musician 29:26, October 1924.
Pert refers to musical compositions as sounding masculine or feminine. The American Mrs. H. H. A. Beach is one of the composers discussed.

246 Petrides, Frederique. "Women in Orchestras." Etude 56:429, July 1938.
Petrides discusses famous women conductors such as Antonia Brico. She also addresses the growth of women's orchestras in America at this time.

247 Peyser, Ethel R. "Some Prima Donnas I Have Known." Musician 34:11-12, May 1929.
Memories of some women opera stars that Ethel Peyser has known, among them the American Martha Attwood.

248 Putnam, A. "Violin Playing As a Profession for Women." Musician 15:57, January 1910.

249 "Qualifications for an Opera Soprano." Musician 22:702, September 1917.

250 Ramsey, Frederic, and Smith, Charles Edward. Jazzmen. St. Clair Shores, Mich.: Scholarly Press, 1972, c1939.
Lil Hardin and Bessie Smith are discussed.

251 Reis, Clair Raphael. American Composers; A Record of Works Written between 1912 and 1932. 2nd ed. New York: International Society for Contemporary Music, United States Section, 1932.
Women composers are included.

252 _____. Composers, Conductors and Critics. New York: Oxford University Press, 1955.
Ms. Reis's remembrances of the League of Composers which she helped found. She was executive chairman for twenty-five years. This organization is a record of contemporary American music of the 1920's and 1930's.

253 Ritter, Mrs. Frances Malone. Woman As a Musician;

An Art-Historical Study. New York: E. Schuberth, 1876.
"Read before the Centennial Congress, in Philadelphia, of the Association for the Advancement of Woman, and published in the Woman's Journal. Here printed with additions."

254 Rogers, Clara Kathleen. Memories of a Musical Career. Boston: Little, Brown and Co., 1919.
Although born in England, she settled in Boston as a singer and teacher. This work is her autobiography.

255 _____. The Story of Two Lives. Norwood, Mass.: n.p., 1932.
A sequel to her Memories of a Musical Career. She made Boston her home following a career as an operatic soprano.

256 Rogers, Francis. Some Famous Singers of the 19th Century. New York: H. W. Gray Co., 1914.
Contents include Maria and Pauline Garcia, Henrietta Sontag, and Jenny Lind.

257 Sachse, Julius Fredrich. Music of the Ephrata Cloister. New York: AMS Press, 1971, c1903.
The Sisters in this German-Pennsylvanian cloister were in the choirs after singing schools were founded, and they composed words and music to some of their hymns.

258 Samaroff Stokowski, Olga. An American Musician's Story. New York: W. W. Norton, 1939.

259 Sargeant, Winthrop. Jazz: Hot and Hybrid. 3rd ed. New York: Da Capo Press, 1975.
A thorough musical analysis of Bessie Smith's style is part of this study of jazz theory.

260 Schoen-René, Anna Eugénie. America's Musical Inheritance; Memories and Reminiscences. New York: G. P. Putnam's Sons, 1941.
She writes about her experiences and impressions of concert life in America. Among her memories are her opinions of other women such as Lilli Lehmann.

261 Scholes, Percy Alfred. Everyman and His Music; Simple Papers on Varied Subjects. Freeport, N.Y.:

Books for Libraries Press, 1969, c1917.
"Reprinted from Everyman, The Evening Standard, and The Music Student." Several chapters are devoted to music in America. Chapter 12 reveals Mrs. Edward MacDowell's great contributions in founding a colony for creative workers.

262 Schuller, Gunther. Early Jazz: Its Roots and Musical Development. New York: Oxford University Press, 1968.
A section within Chapter 5 ("Virtuoso Performers of the Twenties") is devoted to the blues singer Bessie Smith.

263 Schumann-Heink, E. "Girl Who Has a Good Voice." Ladies Home Journal 20:12, October 1903.

264 _____. Where Shall Our Girls Study Music?" Good Housekeeping 60:166-167, February 1915.

265 Scruggs, Lawson Andrew. Women of Distinction: Remarkable in Works and Invincible in Character. Raleigh, N.C.: L. A. Scruggs, 1893.
This book of distinguished Negro women includes Sissieretta Jones, the singer who was active in the concert and theater life of America at this time.

266 Seltsam, William H. Metropolitan Opera Annals; A Chronicle of Artists and Performances. New York: H. W. Wilson, 1947.
This opera house opened in 1888. Photographs, lists of personnel, and excerpts from press reviews are included.

267 Sembrich, M. "Why So Few Girls Succeed As Singers." Ladies Home Journal 27:18, February 1910.

268 "Should a Woman Singer Wear a Corset?" Musician 19:338-339, 410-411, May-June 1914.
A symposium on appropriate clothing for singers.

269 "Should Women Be Allowed to Make a Career in Music?" New Republic 95:263, July 13, 1938.
Most of the nation's orchestras do not include women at this time except as an occasional harpist or organist. A group has been formed to attempt to change this situation.

270 Slonimsky, Nicolas. Music Since 1900. 4th ed. New York: Scribner's Sons, 1971.
Contains a chronology of important musical events 1900-1948 throughout the world. Events concerning American women musicians such as Mrs. H. H. A. Beach are found.

271 Smith, Caroline Estes. The Philharmonic Orchestra of Los Angeles; "The First Decade," 1919-1929. Los Angeles: Press of United Printing Co., 1930.
Information on the Women's Symphony Orchestra of Los Angeles which was organized in 1893 is included. A list of personnel is given plus details of their first concerts.

272 Smith, Charles Edward. "Ma Rainey and the Minstrels." Record Changer 14(6):5-6, 1955.
Gertrude "Ma" Rainey's career as a Negro blues singer is told. She made about sixty records and taught her singing style to a young Memphis girl named Bessie Smith.

273 Smith, Frances M. "Our Women Violinists." Peiferson's Magazine March 1873, pp. 223-234.

274 Smyth, Ethel Mary. Female Pipings in Eden. 2nd ed. London: P. Davies, 1934.
A collection of Smyth's writings, many of which are related to her strong feelings about the competence of women in music.

275 _____. Streaks of Life. New York: A. A. Knopf, 1922.
As an English composer herself, Smyth defends the place of women in music. She feels that women musicians are as capable if not better than men in the field.

276 Snyder, L. "19th-Century Festival--Music by Ms.'s-- and by Masters." Christian Science Monitor 64:8, August 7, 1972.

277 "Solomon's Wives." Time 34:36, October 30, 1939.
Includes information on early development of women's orchestras in the U.S. There were at least twelve orchestras composed entirely of women in the nation during 1939.

278 Spaeth, Sigmund. "It Isn't Sissy to Like Music." *Rotarian* 49:16-19, October 1936.

279 Stanley, M. "Story of Anna Case." *Woman's Home Companion* 45:21, March 1918.

280 Stearns, Marshall Winslow. *The Story of Jazz*. New York: Oxford University Press, 1956.
   A comprehensive account of the evolution of jazz including women who played an important part in this development, such as Bessie Smith.

281 Stevenson, Robert Murrell. *Music in El Paso, 1919-1939*. El Paso: University of Texas at El Paso, 1970.
   Quite a few composers of El Paso were women. This short book discusses the musical scene during the 1920's and 1930's there.

282 Stewart-Baxter, Derrick. *Ma Rainey and the Classic Blues Singers*.
   Ma Rainey and Bessie Smith are the two most important women whose music is discussed in this work.

283 Storer, H. J. "Women As Orchestral Players As Illustrated by the Fadettes." *Musician* 19:511, August 1910.

284 Strange, Lewis Clinton. *Famous Stars of Light Opera*. Boston: L. C. Page, 1907.

285 _____. *Prima Donnas and Soubrettes of Light Opera and Musical Comedy in America*. Boston: L. C. Page, 1900.
   Treats the subject of American actresses and singers of operetta.

286 "Successful Women Song-Writers." *Literary Digest* 55:87, October 13, 1917.
   A number of current popular women composers were interviewed to determine their personal reasons for writing music. Among them are Manna Zucca of Harlem and Elsa Maxwell who composed on the women's rights theme.

287 "Suggestions for Program of Music by American Women." *Musician* 28:28, August 1923.

The Arthur P. Schmidt Publishing Co. has prepared a list of works suitable for a program entirely composed by American women.

288 Sutro, Florence Edith Clinton. Women in Music and Law. New York: Authors' Pub. Co., 1895.
Contains a bibliography of women composers.

289 "Swedish Night." Time 28:41, November 23, 1936.
The Women's Symphony Orchestra of Chicago conducted by Ebba Sundstrom finished its tenth season in 1936. Because of the good reviews and large audiences, it might have been the orchestra's first profitable season.

290 Syford, E. "Recent Songs by American Women Composers." New England Magazine n. s. 48:436-437, 493-495, November-December 1912.

291 Taubman, Hyman Howard. Opera, Front and Back. New York: C. Scribner's Sons, 1938.
Discusses singers and operas at the New York Metropolitan Opera House.

292 Taylor, L. M. "What I Wish for My Daughter." Parents' Magazine 11:19, December 1936.
Interview with Kirsten Flagstad.

293 Tetrazzini, Luisa. My Life of Song. Philadelphia: Dorrance & Co., 1922.
Biography of an Italian coloratura soprano who performed widely in operas and concert tours in the U. S. before World War I.

294 Thomas, D. "That Traipsin' Woman; Jean Thomas, Originator of the American Folk Song Festival." Independent Woman 13:169, June 1934.

295 Thompson, Oscar. The American Singer; A Hundred Years of Success in Opera. New York: Johnson Reprint Corp., 1969, c1937.
An excellent survey of American singers from about the 1830's to the 1930's. The text is filled with details about the many women singers of note during this time, such as Clara Louise Kellogg, Minnie Hauk, and Lillian Nordica.

296 Tick, Judith. "Women As Professional Musicians in the United States, 1870-1900." Yearbook for Inter-American Musical Research 9:95-133, 1973.
   An examination of the changing status of women in music during the thirty years preceding the twentieth century.

297 Trotter, James M. Music and Some Highly Musical People. New York: Johnson Reprint Corp., 1968, c1881.
   Includes "sketches of the lives of remarkable musicians of the colored race ... and copies of music composed by colored men." Negro women musicians are noted as well, such as Elizabeth Taylor Greenfield, Anna and Emma Hyers, and Nellie E. Brown.

298 Turner, C. "Music and the Women's Crusade." Arts and Decoration 19:29, September 1923.

299 Upton, George Putnam. Musical Memories; My Recollections of Celebrities of the Half Century, 1850-1900. Chicago, A. C. McClurg & Co., 1908.
   Among his memories are the concerts of Jenny Lind, Henriette Sontag, Marietta Alboni, Anna Thillon, and Catherine Hayes who are discussed in the first two chapters. As a Chicago music critic, his work is an important historical record of that time.

300 _____. Woman in Music. 6th ed. Chicago: A. C. McClurg & Co., 1899.
   Gives a picture of women's influence on music and the musicians who produced it. Reasons for women's failure to become well-known composers are given.

301 Urmy, C. "Musical Girl's Chances." Ladies Home Journal 33:36, April 1916.

302 "The Voices of Young Girls Should Be under Careful Training." Etude 42:344, May 1924.
   Addresses the problem of the girl's voice from age twelve to fourteen. It was suggested that the voice should not be forced since the individual has not reached maturity. Frequent lessons are unnecessary at this age, but there is no reason that a young girl should not have voice training.

303 Wack, Harry Wellington. "Singers of the Century."

Overland Monthly s2 25:339-348, April 1895.
Prominent women singers are discussed, most of whom sang in the U.S. at some point in their careers. Ellen Beach Yaw was considered one of the most promising American singers of the time according to this article.

304 Wagenknecht, Edward Charles. Geraldine Farrar; An Authorized Record. Seattle: University Book Store, 1929.
A biography of this famous singer of the early 1900's.

305 Wagnalls, Mabel. Opera and Its Stars. New York: Funk & Wagnalls Co., 1924.
This is an amplification of Wagnalls's Stars of the Opera. In addition to information about the music and stories of some of the greatest operas, there are "a series of interviews with the world's famous sopranos." Nellie Melba and Lillian Nordica are two of the sopranos interviewed.

306 _____. Stars of the Opera. New York: Funk & Wagnalls Co., 1899.
"A description of operas & a series of personal interviews with Marcella Sembrich, Emma Eames, Emma Calvê, Lillian Nordica, Lilli Lehmann, & Nellie Melba."

307 Ware, H. "Motherhood and Careers: or, The Mother Artist." Musician 21:728, December 1916.

308 Warren, J. "Women Who Are Making a Musical America." Delineator 76:164, September 1910.

309 Watkins, M. F. "In the Kingdom of Gatti-Casazza." Pictorial Review 27:2, March 1926.

310 Wechsberg, Joseph. Red Plush and Black Velvet; The Story of Melba and Her Times. Boston: Little, Brown and Co., 1961.
The Australian Nellie Melba's biography including information on her concerts in America.

311 Weilich, L. "From Typist to Prima Donna." Etude 56:20, January 1938.
An interview with the Franco-Russian contralto

Sigrid Onegin. She urged young singers to seek musical careers if they feel qualified and not to settle for lesser goals. As an office worker she earned her way to a music career. She considered her former job very beneficial as training for living.

312 "What Geraldine Farrar Would Do If 'Broke.'" <u>Literary Digest</u> 60:68-76, February 15, 1919.
    Miss Farrar, an opera singer, dispelled the myth that achieving success in opera is luxurious and romantic. She also states that she would make up her mind to do well in whatever profession she might choose.

313 "When Women Blow Horns." <u>Literary Digest</u> 113:19-20, April 2, 1932.
    The National Women's Symphony Orchestra of Boston had its debut with Ethel Leginska as conductor. The review of the first performance was quite favorable. The confidence and businesslike manner of the group showed a professionalism which should have helped other women's orchestras to be received favorably by the public.

314 "Where Women Do Not Lead." <u>Literary Digest</u> 59:25, December 21, 1918.
    Women composers have generally been considered less talented than men. In 1918 Lilli Boulanger was being heralded as the greatest woman composer in music history.

315 Willard, Frances Elizabeth, and Livermore, Mary A. <u>A Woman of the Century: Fourteen Hundred-Seventy Biographical Sketches Accompanied by Portraits of Leading American Women in All Walks of Life.</u> Buffalo: C. W. Moulton, 1893.
    Includes a number of notable women musicians such as Mrs. Kate J. Brainard and Mrs. Dora Hennings.

316 Williams, Katherine. "What I See in the Future for the Girl Musician." <u>School Musician</u> 44:423, January 1973.
    Reprinted from a 1934 issue of <u>School Musician</u>. This is a chronicle of the musical life of one of America's foremost woman trumpeters. She was gratified by the opportunities which were opening up for women instrumentalists at this time.

317 Wilson, A. "Mrs. H. H. A. Beach; A Conversation on Musical Conditions in America." Musician 17:9-10, January 1912.

318 "Woman and Music; Twin Souls of Civilization." Etude 47:793, November 1929.
An editorial on the importance of music in a woman's life, not as a vocation, but for happiness and solace.

319 "Woman's Orchestra Makes Its Debut." Commonweal 21:512, March 1, 1935.
Over 2000 concert-goers heard the first performance of the Women's Symphony of New York conducted by Antonia Brico in New York City's Town Hall. It is the first attempt of this nature since Ethel Leginska's orchestra many years before.

320 "Women As Musicians." Etude 42:166, March 1924.
A review of Dr. Ethel Smyth's book, Streaks of Life, which defends women's place in the music profession. She was a well-known composer in England and felt that the music world was suffering because of the lack of women in the field.

321 "Women in the Orchestra." Literary Digest 52:504-505, February 26, 1916.
Leopold Stokowski, one of America's leading orchestra conductors, felt that women musicians could be a beneficial addition to symphonies. However, he was doubtful about women being able to endure the physical rigors of conducting an entire opera.

322 "Women on Their Own; Chicago Woman's Symphony Orchestra." Time 26:52, December 16, 1935.
This all-female symphony was organized ten years ago by three ladies who wished to participate in an orchestra. They have gained popularity during the past six years with Ebba Sundstrom as their conductor.

323 Wood, Peggy. "I Remember Emma." Opera News 35:26-29, February 6, 1971.
Ms. Wood, a Broadway and film actress, recalls her music teacher Emma Calvé who insisted on realistic costumes in the Metropolitan Opera around the 1900's.

324 Wood, V. "Little Hymn Singer." Missionary Review

of the World 62:98, February 1939.
Marian Anderson is discussed.

325 Work, John Wesley. Folk Song of the American Negro.
New York: Negro Universities Press, 1969, c1915.
A few Negro women are discussed in relation to specific folk songs. One example is "Swing Low, Sweet Chariot" composed by Mrs. Sarah Hannah Sheppard.

326 Writers' Program. California. An Anthology of Music Criticism. San Francisco: Writers' Program of the Work Project Administration, 1942.
Writings of music critics are examined in this anthology of reviews from the years 1850-1940 chiefly in the San Francisco area. Articles on many women performers are included.

327 Wurm, Marie. "Woman's Struggle for Recognition in Music." Etude 54:687, November 1936.
Miss Wurm's opinions of the role women have played during the past few centuries in gaining recognition. Among those discussed are Lillian Nordica who toured in the U.S.

328 Yaw, Ellen Beach. "To Girls Who Want to Sing."
Delineator 73:130-131, 462, 600, January; March-April 1909.

4

ROSIE THE RIVETER AND
THE WOMEN'S LIBERATION MOVEMENT (1939-1976)

329 Abel, Mrs. I. "Women's Association Fund Raising Projects." American Symphony Orchestra League Newsletter 20(3-4):23, June-November 1969.

330 Adams, John Clarke. "Song of Yesteryear." Opera News 38:12-17, February 9, 1974.
Bel canto singing of the past is contrasted with the opera singers' present-day style of singing. Women such as Adelina Patti and Maria Callas are discussed.

331 "Admirer's Kiss for a Beloved Teacher." Life 52:42, February 23, 1962.
Leonard Bernstein attended Nadia Boulanger's 75th birthday celebration. Among her well-known pupils are the Americans Bernstein, Virgil Thomson, Aaron Copland, and Roger Sessions.

332 Albus, Harry James. The "Deep River" Girl; The Life of Marian Anderson in Story Form. Grand Rapids, Mich.: W. B. Eerdmans Pub. Co., 1949.
A biography of this Negro singer who was the first of her race to be signed to sing at the Metropolitan Opera.

333 Alexander, Lucille Dillinger. "A Double Career--Band Directing and Marriage; Is It Possible? Is It Advisable?" School Musician 43:58-59, April 1972.
This woman band director encourages women students to combine marriage and a career as a band director only if they are very ambitious. She described some of the pitfalls of pursuing such a busy schedule.

334 Alterman, Loraine. "Judy in Disguise." Melody Maker 48:10-11, September 1, 1973.

335 _____. "Musical Composition: Is It for Men Only?" Hi Fi/Stereo Review 16:68-72, February 1966.

336 _____. "Rock and Roll Women." Melody Maker 47:51, October 14, 1972.

337 Altman, Thelma. "The Neglected Contralto." Music Journal 8:15, November 1950.
 Today's composers tend to neglect the contralto voice or to relegate it to a secondary role in favor of the soprano. At times in the past the contralto received much acclaim.

338 "American Accordionists Name Belfiore Pres.--1st Woman." Music Trades 119:50, February 1971.

339 "American Composers." Music Clubs Magazine 52(3):4, 1973.
 Women are included in this list of American composers.

340 Anderson, Marian. My Lord, What a Morning; An Autobiography. New York: Viking Press, 1956.
 Marian Anderson was the first black to be involved regularly in the New York Metropolitan Opera performances. Her autobiography traces her musical beginnings from special performances in church services while in grade school through her years of concert appearances.

341 "Anderson in Baltimore." Musical America 73:12, November 15, 1953.
 Baltimore's Lyric Theatre permitted only white performers on its stage until 1954, when it granted permission for Marian Anderson to sing there.

342 Angelou, M. "Nina Simone: High Priestess of Soul." Redbook 136:77, November 1970.

343 "Another Distaff Victory." Diapason 60:14, July 1969.
 Recently in 1969 Barbara Kolb, a New York organist, received the American Prix de Rome. The article also relates other activities in which women have gained prominence.

344 Apel, Paul Hermann. Music of the Americas, North and South. New York: Vantage Press, 1958.

Includes information on music of both North and South America. One section of "Music of North America" is devoted to women who compose songs and instrumental music, pp. 151-155. Short biographical sketches are given for musicians such as Mrs. H. H. A. Beach, Harriet Ware, and Peggy Glanville-Hicks.

345 Appleton, Jane Scovell. "Sarah Caldwell: The Flamboyant of the Opera." Ms. 3:26, May 1975.
An in-depth interview with the conductor Sarah Caldwell.

346 Ardoin, John. Callas: The Art and the Life. New York: Holt, Rinehart and Winston, 1974.
Also included in this book about Maria Callas's career in opera is Gerald Fitzgerald's work The Great Years.

347 _____. "Visit from Mademoiselle." Musical America 82:63, April 1962.
The Frenchwoman Nadia Boulanger briefly lectured at the Manhattan School of Music and spoke with many aspiring composers. She has been an important influence on American music and has been the teacher of many famous American musicians.

348 Arell, Ruth. "Muscle Men & Maids of Music." Music Journal 8:22, November 1950.
Although music has sometimes been considered a "sissy" occupation by some, many well-known male and female musicians have been quite athletic to keep fit physically for their performances.

349 _____. "Tin Pan Alley Sallys; Women Who Write Popular Songs." Independent Woman 19:350, November 1940.

350 Arlyck, Diana Miller. "Piano Teacher Speaks Her Mind." Parents' Magazine 27:36-37, January 1952.
Suggestions for parents on ways to increase their children's chances of being successful in music.

351 Arment, Hollace Elbert. "A Study by Means of Spectrographic Analysis of the Brightness and Darkness Qualities of Vowel Tones in Women's Voices." Ed. D. dissertation, Indiana University, 1960.

352 Armsby, Leonora Wood. We Shall Have Music. San Francisco: Pisani Print. & Pub. Co., 1960.
   She "directed the rising fortunes of the Musical Association of San Francisco as the sponsoring organization for the symphony...." A musician herself, Armsby did much to make the orchestra become a prominent part of communities from 1935-1953.

353 Armstrong, Donald Jan. "A Study of Some Important Twentieth Century Secular Compositions for Women's Chorus with a Preliminary Discussion of Secular Choral Music from a Historical and Philosophical Viewpoint." D.M.A. dissertation, University of Texas at Austin, 1968.

354 Aronowitz, Alfred G. "Swinging Nuns." Saturday Evening Post 237:66-67, January 4, 1964.
   One of the nation's best selling records during 1964 was "Dominique" which was part of a nun's album entitled "The Singing Nun."

355 _____ and Blonsky, Marshall. "Three's Company: Peter, Paul & Mary." Saturday Evening Post 237:30, May 30, 1964.
   Mary Travers is an integral part of this folk music trio. The article is an interview with them.

356 Ashley, Patricia, and Handly, Donna. "Here They Are--on a Plastic Platter; With Discography." Ms. 4:111, November 1975.
   Reviews of several recent recordings of works by women composers including Mrs. H.H.A. Beach (Amy Marcy Cheney Beach). Also, the available discography of the works of forty-six women is listed at the end.

357 Asklund, Gunnar. "Preparing for an Operatic Career." Etude 72:15, February 1954.
   An interview with Camilla William, a black woman from Virginia. She noted that the famous opera star Geraldine Farrar made her acutely aware of voice quality in operatic singing.

358 _____. "Singing in the Movies." Etude 70:16, November 1952.
   An interview with Kathryn Grayson, a popular singing actress. She gives advice to those who wish to follow a singing career in films.

359 "At the Drinkers." Newsweek 31:69, February 2, 1948.
Harry and Sophie Drinker of Philadelphia often had serious music lovers visiting at their home. Mrs. Drinker's recent book Music and Women illustrated her liberated position on women in music.

360 Atkinson, N. "The Repertoire for Female Voices." Musical Opinion 89:723, September 1966.

361 "Attention, Women Composers!" Musical Newsletter 44:14, May 1952.
Notice of the Delta Omicron (International Organization of Women Musicians) composition contest.

362 "Available Recordings of Works by Women Composers." High Fidelity/Musical America 23:53, February 1973.
Twenty-nine women composers are listed with available recordings of each. Among them are a number of Americans such as Peggy Glanville-Hicks and Ruth Crawford Seeger.

363 Avery, Paul. "Mildred Harrison's Viet Nam Ordeal." Ebony 22:88, May 1967.
Harrison, a black jazz singer, was entertaining servicemen when she suddenly was denied permission to leave the country.

364 "Awards Presented for Symphony Women's Associations' 'Most Significant Projects' for 1967-1968." American Symphony Orchestra League Newsletter 19(3):5, 1968.
Each local association reported on its most valuable project related to the community and its orchestra. The best projects were listed.

365 "BMI's Feminine Touch." Variety 206:2, May 29, 1957.

366 "Baby, Baby, Where Did Diana Go?" Time 96:30-31, August 17, 1970.
Diana Ross of the Supremes is discussed.

367 Baer, B. "New Soul-Sound." Look 32:M8-10, February 20, 1968.
Aretha Franklin's gospel rock is reviewed. She divulged her philosophy of life and defined "soul."

368 Baez, Joan. Daybreak. New York: Dial Press, 1968.
An autobiography of this folk singer's life and career.

369 Bailey, Pearl. <u>The Raw Pearl</u>. New York: Harcourt, Brace & World, 1968.
    Pearl Bailey's account of her childhood and her success in show business in such productions as <u>Porgy and Bess</u> and St. Louis Blues.

370 _____. <u>Talking to Myself</u>. New York: Harcourt Brace Jovanovich, 1971.
    Essays by the black singer-entertainer Pearl Bailey. Among her reminiscences are poems, prayers, and feelings about her experiences in life. Some of the material in <u>The Raw Pearl</u> is repeated here, she concedes, but with different insights.

371 Baird, Pat. "Fanny: All Woman, All Rock and Roll." <u>Senior Scholastic</u> 100:32-34, April 24, 1972.
    This four-member female rock group enjoys playing together and they feel that they have good talent. They attribute some of their acceptance and success to the Women's Liberation Movement.

372 Baker, David. "Female Accompanists." <u>Musical America</u> 70:14, October 1950.
    A letter to the editor decrying the practice of discrimination against women as accompanists for the best singers. Men usually are selected to accompany prominent singers.

373 Ballard, P. "Little Girls, Take It Away!" <u>Variety</u> 221:210, January 4, 1961.
    Popular songs are discussed in relation to female vocalists.

374 Balliett, Whitney. <u>Dinosaurs in the Morning; 41 Pieces on Jazz</u>. Philadelphia: J. B. Lippincott Co., 1962.
    Forty-one essays on jazz which first appeared in <u>The New Yorker</u> from 1957-1962. One of the sections is devoted to Billie Holiday, the blues singer.

375 _____. <u>Ecstasy at the Onion; Thirty-one Pieces on Jazz</u>. Indianapolis: Bobbs-Merrill Co., 1971.
    A collection of articles which first appeared in <u>The New Yorker</u>. None is exclusively about women, but some singers such as Mahalia Jackson are mentioned in various articles.

376 _____. <u>New York Notes; A Journal of Jazz 1972-1975</u>. Boston: Houghton Mifflin, 1976.

Some of these articles first appeared in The New Yorker. Only the most important events in jazz are included, among them Mahalia Jackson's death, and the reemergence of such women jazz musicians as Helen Humes and Anita Ellis.

377 _____. Such Sweet Thunder; Forty-nine Pieces on Jazz. Indianapolis: Bobbs-Merrill Co., 1966.
These articles originally appeared in The New Yorker between 1962 and 1966. One of these sections is entitled "The Ladies." Critiques of the musical style and recordings of such women as Billie Holiday and Mildred Bailey are among them.

378 Barnes, Nancy. "Women in Music: A Preliminary Report." College Music Symposium 14:67-70, 1974.
A report of the statistics available on the women faculty and students in colleges. Although women comprise the majority of music students as undergraduates and graduates, the percentage of professional women in music is extremely small in comparison.

379 "A Barrier Is Broken." Musical America 74:4, November 1, 1954.
The Metropolitan Opera Association of New York for the first time has permitted a black person on the roster of one of its operas. Marian Anderson has broken this tradition by singing an important role in Verdi's A Masked Ball.

380 Bart, Teddy. Inside Music City, U.S.A. Nashville: Aurora, 1970.
Interviews with songwriters of the Nashville sound. One chapter is "Marijohn Wilkin: Is the Music Business More Difficult for Women?" Ms. Wilkin's conclusion is that women with talent can be successful in the creative world, and there are many ladies writing songs in Nashville. In addition, she feels that women are treated more as equals in music than in most other professions.

381 Barzun, Jacques. Music in American Life. Gloucester, Mass.: P. Smith, 1958, c1956.
This short study is Barzun's view of the part that music plays in American life. Several women financial supporters of musical organizations are in the chapter on "The Trade," such as Elsie Eckstein and

her gift of $4,200,000 to the Northwestern University School of Music.

382 "Batoners Hit 'Union Musicians Only' Tag in Casting Call for Gal Tooters." <u>Variety</u> 242:193, May 4, 1966.

383 "Beacon." <u>Newsweek</u> 65:87-88, April 26, 1965.
Marian Anderson's career is noted. Among her achievements is being the first Negro to sing at the Metropolitan Opera.

384 Becker, Paula. <u>Let the Song Go On; Fifty Years of Gospel Singing with the Speer Family</u>. Nashville: Impact Books, 1971.
The three women and four men of the Alabama Speer family were prominent evangelistic singers during the first half of the twentieth century. Their children are now carrying on the tradition.

385 Beckley, Paul V. "Divas in Movieland." <u>Opera News</u> 29:8-13, December 19, 1964.
An examination of American films which were made of operas or incorporated operatic elements. Mary Garden is one of the most well-known opera singers to be involved in movies.

386 Behrens, E. "The Federation's Godchildren." <u>Music Clubs Magazine</u> 33:4, January 1954.
Some solutions are offered for the problems musicians face in combining careers and parenthood.

387 Belz, Carl. <u>The Story of Rock</u>. 2nd ed. New York: Oxford University Press, 1972.
Women who were important in the history of rock and roll music from 1954-1971 are discussed along with male musicians.

388 Bender, W. "Janis and Jimi, Op. Posth." <u>Time</u> 97:76, February 15, 1971.
Janis Joplin and Jimi Hendrix both died from drugs while they were successful in their careers as rock musicians.

389 _____. "Sarah's Women: New York Philharmonic Concert." <u>Time</u> 106:88, November 24, 1975.
Sarah Caldwell the conductor is discussed.

390 Bergman, Nancy. "Women Can Sing Barbershop." Music Journal 16:30, November-December 1958.
Women as well as men are now enjoying singing in barbershop quartets. The Sweet Adelines, founded in 1947, is helping promote women's interest in this type of harmony and has gained 7,000 members by 1958.

391 "Bermuda Belles." Newsweek 39:90, February 18, 1952.
The Bell Sisters, Cynthia and Kay Strother, are young ladies who have just recorded their first hit record "Bermuda."

392 Bernard, S. "Rock Giants from A-Z; Carole King: From Teen Love to Superstar." Melody Maker 49: 25-26, January 19, 1974.

393 "Best-Seller Disk Battle of Sexes Finds Femmes Way Out in Front." Variety 186:42, May 21, 1952.

394 Bims, Hamilton. "Felicia Weathers: Dauntless Diva." Ebony 25:52, May 1970.
This black soprano has followed in the footsteps of opera stars such as Leontyne Price and Marian Anderson.

395 Bing, Rudolf. 5000 Nights at the Opera. Garden City, N.Y.: Doubleday, 1972.
Mr. Bing recalls many of his experiences as manager of the New York Metropolitan Opera with such prima donnas as the American Marian Anderson.

396 Birnie, W. A. "How's Your Umph? Al Siegel Tells How to Put Over a Song and Be a Glamour Girl." American Magazine 127:28, February 1939.

397 Block, Adrienne Fried. "The Woman Musician on Campus: Hiring and Promotion Patterns." High Fidelity/Musical America 25:MA22-23, June 1975.
Statistics of numbers of women receiving degrees plus percentages of women on music faculties are given.

398 _____. "Women in the Profession in Higher Education." College Music Symposium 14:60-66, 1974.
Legislation eliminating sex discrimination in faculty hiring should increase the percentage of women teach-

ing music in colleges and universities. Many statistics are included which substantiate the low number of women faculty.

399 Bloomfield, Arthur J. 50 Years of the San Francisco Opera. San Francisco Book Co., 1972.
The volume is an expanded version of the earlier work: The San Francisco Opera, 1923-61. This is a detailed chronicle of the history of the organization with many anecdotes. Information on many of the performers such as Leontyne Price is included.

400 "Blues for Janis." Time 96:54, October 19, 1970.
Janis Joplin, the blues singer, is discussed.

401 "Bobbie's Billie's Bundle." Time 89:50-51, September 1, 1967.
Bobbie Gentry is the subject.

402 Boeckman, Charles. And the Beat Goes On; A Survey of Pop Music in America. Washington, D.C.: R. B. Luce, 1972.
Many women are included in this overview of popular music in all areas of popular music.

403 "Bohemian Girl Songs Mingle with Moose in Iowa." Newsweek 5:30, June 29, 1935.
The 4-H club girls of Iowa wanted to stage a musical as part of their music appreciation training at their June convention. Adults played the leading roles, but the 5,000 4-H girls filled the part of minor characters and the chorus of The Bohemian Girl.

404 Bond, V. "Closet Composers: A Portrait of Doriana Gray." Instrumental Music 74:7, July 1975.

405 "Boston's New First Flutist." Woodwind Magazine 5:16, October 1952.
Doroit Anthony recently became the first chair flutist of the Boston Symphony and was the first woman to be selected for a solo desk capacity. Ann De Guichard, a bassoonist, earlier became the first woman member of Boston's Symphony.

406 Bowen, C. D. "Mother, Learn Your Notes." Woman's Home Companion 67:8, June 1940.

407 Bowen, Jean. "Women in Music--Their Fair Share?" High Fidelity/Musical America 24:MA20, August 1974.
A colloquium was held to discuss women in the music profession during 1974. During the study statistics were given showing the small ratio of women to men in selected areas of music. Suggestions were made to correct this condition.

408 Brand, Oscar. The Ballad Mongers; Rise of the Modern Folksong. New York: Funk & Wagnalls, 1962.
A number of women have had an influence on folk music, such as Joan Baez and Jean Ritchie.

409 Branscombe, G. "The Sound of Trumpets." Showcase 41(3):8-10, 1962.

410 Brant, LeRoy V. "The Amazing Versatility of American Singers." Etude 71:11, June 1953.
An interview with Blanche Thebom who is a principal singer at the Metropolitan opera.

411 "Brash Bess Is on Her Way." Newsweek 88:119, October 11, 1976.
Clamma Dale is a Negro singer who is becoming more popular in 1976.

412 Briggs, John. "Onstage: The Prima Donna." New York Times Magazine November 11, 1956, p. 16.
Rudolph Bing, the manager of the Metropolitan Opera, has been working with many divas such as Maria Callas. Some of the temperamental antics of Callas and others are related.

413 _____. Requiem for a Yellow Brick Brewery; A History of the Metropolitan Opera. Boston: Little, Brown, 1969.
Includes information and pictures of many Metropolitan Opera prima donnas who are Americans, such as Leontyne Price and Maria Callas.

414 Briggs, Marion L. "Breaking a Boston Symphony Tradition." Etude 72:13, September 1954.
Doriot Anthony has recently become the first chair flutist in the Boston Symphony Orchestra. She was the first woman to achieve the status of principal chair in this organization.

415 "Broadway's Newest Star." Ebony 17:42, July 1962.
Diahann Carroll stars in the Richard Rodgers musical No Strings.

416 Brook, Donald. Singers of Today. London: Rockliff, 1949.
About half of these short biographies of singers are about women, but none is about Americans. However, several of them traveled to the United States and sang in operas here.

417 "Brooklyn Girl Wins Composition Award." Musical America 73:17, April 1, 1953.
The fifth annual composition contest of the New York Philharmonic's Young People's Concerts has been won by a fifteen-year-old girl. Dorothy Hill's piano solo was played in the final Young People's Concert of the season.

418 Brooks, Benjamin. "How of Creative Composition." Etude 61:151, March 1943.
Mrs. H. H. A. Beach, one of early America's foremost composers, tells about her methods of composition. Most of her work was accomplished through trial and error.

419 Brown, Geoff. "Where Have All the Good Girls Gone?" Melody Maker 49:38-39, March 30, 1974.

420 Bryant, Anita. Amazing Grace. Old Tappan, N.J.: F. H. Revelle Co., 1971.
The story of Anita Bryant's singing career.

421 _____. Mine Eyes Have Seen the Glory. New York: Bantam, 1976.
Anita Bryant shares her religious experiences.

422 Bucci, Jerry Michael. "Love, Marriage, and Family Life Themes in the Popular Song: A Comparison of the Years 1940 and 1965." Ed.D. dissertation, Columbia University, 1968.

423 Buehlman, Barbara. "Should a Woman Be a Band Director?" Instrumentalist 21:56, September 1966.
Buehlman attempts to answer the question of whether or not a woman can be a successful band director. She suggests the following criteria in

determining a woman's ability: musical talent, administrative ability, personality, and intelligence. A little luck is the only other thing a woman needs.

424 Bundy, June. "Gals Across Nation Are Grabbing Mikes to Gab on Deejay Shows." Billboard 68:14, January 7, 1956.

425 _____. "Gals Take a Beating in Album Sales but Hold Their Own in Singles Mkt." Billboard Music Week 74:4, March 3, 1962.

426 Butler, Blanche. "The Only Ladies' Bagpipe Band in America." Etude 59:10, January 1941.
   Los Angeles is the home of an all-female bagpipe band in 1941. Details of its rehearsals and activities are given.

427 Butterfield, H. M. "Interesting the Teen-age Girl." Etude 60:419, June 1942.
   Specific suggestions for the music teacher to use to retain the interest of teen-age girls in their musical studies.

428 Cage, Ruth. "Rhythm & Blues." Down Beat 22:27, June 15, 1955.
   Apathy toward female popular singers is evident from the small percentage of records produced by them.

429 Cahoon, Helen Fouts. "Popular Singers Can Be Taught." Music Journal 16:6-7, February 1958.
   Ms. Cahoon was the vocal teacher who coached Mary Martin and the Andrews Sisters. She stressed the real need for proper vocal techniques for popular singers since they often have grueling schedules of rehearsals, recording sessions, and frequent appearances while on tour.

430 Callas, Evangelia. My Daughter--Maria Callas. London: Leslie Frewin, 1967.
   A biography of the prima donna Maria Callas. The emphasis is on her life other than her career as a singer.

431 Callas, Maria. "Processo Alla Callas: Bel Canto Style." New Yorker 47:31-32, April 24, 1971.

An interview with the great soprano who was born in New York and has performed in operas all over the world.

432 Calton, David. Janis. New York: Simon and Schuster, 1971.
Interviews with Janis Joplin and people who knew her. A large section is devoted to photographs of her and to reproductions of the blues and rock music she sang.

433 Calvin, S. "Missing Women: On the Voodoo Trail to Jazz." Journal of Jazz Studies 3(1):4-27, 1975.

434 Cantwell, Jean Barker. "Observations on Female Musicians." Woodwind World 3:4-5, 1960.
Cantwell, a former oboist with the Chicago Women's Symphony, discusses her feelings about the difficulties of women combining a music career and marriage. She suggests concentrating on being a good housewife first, and a musician second.

435 Caracappa, Michael. "Wonder Woman of 42nd Street." Music Journal 24:18, May 1966.
Lee Wurlitzer of the New York Wurlitzer firm managed to make the world's largest purchase of rare violins. Details of the negotiations and her shrewdness despite her lack of negotiating experience in this area are divulged.

436 Cardus, Neville. Kathleen Ferrier, 1912-1953; A Memoir. London: H. Hamilton, 1955.
An English contralto who became a very popular opera star all over the world. Information on her American tours and her experiences here are included.

437 "Carly Simon Joins the Ladies." Melody Maker 46:27, May 15, 1971.

438 "Carol Carmichael Boosts Females as Producers." Billboard 86:4, May 4, 1974.
Carol Carmichael, a Los Angeles based independent record producer, feels more women should get into the record business. She claims that women are better organized and are able to handle budgets more realistically.

439 "Carolyn Leigh's 'Little Me' Lyrics Accent Femme Cleffers' B'way Role." Variety 228:1, November 21, 1962.

440 Casale, Giac. "Five of the World's Leading Singers of Opera Portrayed in Five Resplendent Roles." Look 26:39, February 27, 1962.
Maria Callas in Norma, Leontyne Price in Aïda, and Anna Moffo in La Traviata are briefly discussed in their respective roles.

441 Celli, Teodoro. "Great Artists of Our Time." Saturday Review 42:40, January 31, 1959.
Maria Meneghini Callas is discussed in this lengthy article, which examines the qualities that make her a great singer.

442 "Chicks in the Chart." Melody Maker 40:8, January 30, 1965.

443 Chilton, John. Billie's Blues: Billie Holiday's Story, 1933-1959. New York: Stein and Day, 1975.
A biography of this black blues singer plus an analysis of her recorded songs.

444 Chotzinoff, Samuel. "Conversation with Leontyne Price." Holiday 35:103, March 1964.
An in-depth interview with this black opera star who tells of her childhood and the development of her career.

445 Christgau, Georgia. "Does the Women's Movement Have a Sense of Rhythm?" Ms. 4:39, December 1975.
A National Women's Music Festival was held June 10-15, 1975, at the University of Illinois, Champaign. Christgau felt that the concerts, jam sessions, and workshops lacked quality and that the discussions always ended up on the subject of feminism instead of music.

446 _____. "Terry Garthwaite: Cookin' on Her Own." Ms. 5:42, September 1976.
Terry Garthwaite's rock band, the Joy of Cooking, was one of the first all-female rock bands until it broke up in 1973. This interview with the leader examines her career and changing style of singing.

447 "Clamma Dale, Soprano." High Fidelity/Musical America 26:MA25-26, August 1976.
    A review of the young black soprano Clamma Dale at an Alice Tully Hall concert.

448 Clark, Robert S. "Learning from Callas." Stereo Review 28:50-54, March 1972.
    Maria Callas, one of the world's great sopranos, is teaching classes to the best students at New York's Juilliard School of Music. Her classes were attended by Clark who critiques her work with aspiring singers.

449 Cohen, John. "Joan Baez." Sing Out 13:5-7, Summer 1963.
    An evaluation of Joan Baez's style of singing folk music and information about the development of her career.

450 Cole, Mrs. Nat King. "Why I Am Returning to Show Business." Ebony 21:45, January 1966.
    Mrs. Cole discusses her reasons for deciding to return to show business as a singer after the death of her famous husband.

451 Coleman, Emily. "Deathless Diva Carries On!" Theatre Arts 41:86, January 1957.
    An essay which asserts that there is no "rebirth of the prima donna" as many believe. Coleman feels that great women opera stars have always been with us.

452 _____. "Girl of the Golden Voice." New York Times Magazine October 15, 1961, p. 37.
    Leontyne Price is the first Negro to open a season at the New York Metropolitan Opera. An account of her career is given, from her childhood in Mississippi to her Metropolitan opening in The Girl of the Golden West.

453 _____. "What Makes a Prima Donna?" Newsweek 57:63-64, February 13, 1961.
    "Coleman draws a composite portrait of what prima donnas are like today." The temperamental antics of singers of the past have been replaced with a businesslike attitude.

454 Coleman, Henry, and West, Hilda. Girls' Choirs. London: Oxford University Press, 1962.

Directions for the formation, rehearsals and concerts of all-female choirs of secondary school age.

455 Collier, Graham. Inside Jazz. London: Quartet Books, 1973.
In Section Two, on "The Performers," reasons for the small number of women in jazz are given. Some problems that marriages encounter when the husband is a jazz musician are listed as well.

456 Collins, ElVera, and Deiro, Pietro. "Accordian As a Suitable Instrument for Ladies." Etude 57:341, May 1939.
There is a demand for accomplished accordian performers according to this article. Many reasons are listed as to why the accordian is a desirable instrument for a young lady to master.

457 Collins, Judy. "Take the Lilies and the Lace; A Memoir." McCalls 97:66, April 1970.
This is an excerpt from the Judy Collins Songbook. This folk singer tells of her life as she grew up and began singing professionally. She feels her first responsibility is as a mother and her career comes second.

458 Collis, J. "From Where I Sit; Women in Orchestras." Symphony 3:6, October 1949.

459 "Columbus Symphony Expansion under an All-Woman Board of Directors." Symphony Orchestra League Newsletter 8:4, February-March 1957.

460 Commanday, Robert. "San Francisco: The Symphony Scandal." High Fidelity/Musical America 24:MA28-29, September 1974.
When two of the members of the San Francisco Orchestra were fired a great uproar developed. One of them was Elayne Jones, a woman timpanist who was the only Negro to hold a major position in this orchestra. Charges of discrimination were heard and the case will be decided in court.

461 _____. "Women Composers: A Place to Stand; A Worthy Effort Falters." High Fidelity/Musical America 25:MA23, January 1975.
The Cabrillo Music Festival held at Aptos, California, in August of 1974 was designed to bring women's

compositions to the attention of the world. Unfortunately, the music chosen to be presented at this event was not of superior quality, according to this music critic. It therefore made little impression on the public.

462 Contos, Catherine. "Brava, Maestra!" High Fidelity/Musical America 21:MA7-10, May 1971.
An overview of women who have been conductors and some who are currently working in this field around the world. Contos cites some of the problems women face in attempting to follow a career in this field.

463 "Contralto Talks about "Ballad-Huntin'." Musical Courier 141:25, January 1, 1950.
Discussion of North Carolina folk music.

464 Cook, Faith Reyher. "Any Mother Can Sing Better than Lily Pons." Parents' Magazine 22:28-29, November 1947.
Mothers are admonished to sing to their children for their own and for their children's enjoyment.

465 Coon, Caroline. "Rock Musicians Have Much in Common with Bunny Girls." Melody Maker 49:42, June 15, 1974.

466 Copland, Aaron. "Nadia Boulanger, an Affectionate Portrait." Harper's Magazine 221:49, October 1960.
An excerpt from Copland on Music to be published later in 1960. Copland reminisces about his study with Nadia Boulanger, his Parisian composition teacher. Boulanger has had a definite impact on American music through her instruction of Copland and several other well-known American musicians.

467 Coppage, Noel. "Country Music's Traipsin' Women." Stereo Review 33:84-89, December 1974.
A discussion of a number of women who are active in country music. Among those whose style is noted are Loretta Lynn, Tammy Wynette, and Olivia Newton-John.

468 _____. "Troubadettes, Troubadoras, and Troubadines." Stereo Review 29:58-61, September 1972.
Coppage discusses some of the problems popular

female singers suffer in the music business. Among the "troubadettes" (female singers who write their own material) are Carole King, Joni Mitchell, and Grace Slick.

469 Cornell, Helen Loftin. "An Evaluation of Vocal Music by American Women Composers As to Its Appropriateness in the Elementary School." Ph.D. dissertation, Ohio State University, 1973.
A study designed to select works "which would be appropriate to grades four, five and six...." The evaluation concludes that there is ample material written by American women which is available for nine to eleven year olds.

470 Cornish, Nellie Centennial. Miss Aunt Nellie; The Autobiography of Nellie C. Cornish. Seattle: University of Washington Press, 1964.
Miss Cornish was responsible for founding a successful school of the arts in Seattle.

471 "Country Music Gets Soul." Ebony 25:66, March 1970.
Women "soul" singers are branching out into country music.

472 Craig, M. "Women at Work." Musical Courier 153:6, January 15, 1956.

473 Crichton, Kyle Samuel. Subway to the Met: Risë Stevens' Story. Garden City, N.Y.: Doubleday, 1959.
An American mezzo-soprano who performed at the Metropolitan Opera and subsequently sang on the radio, in motion pictures, and on television.

474 Crider, E. O. "San Antonio." Musical Courier 157: 34, May 1958.
Nanette Levi of San Antonio became the first woman concertmaster in the U.S.

475 Cross, D. "The Callas Silliness." Hi-Fi Music at Home 5:19, February 1959.
Discussion of the opera singer Maria Callas.

476 Cuff, J. "Madame President." Ragtimer May-June 1972, pp. 4-5.
Idamay MacInnes heads the Ragtime Society in 1972.

477 Cushing, Mary Watkins. "A Complexity of Gypsies." Opera News 24:4, February 6, 1960.
   A discussion of various singers who sang the role of Carmen over the years at the Metropolitan Opera.

478 Dachs, David. Anything Goes: The World of Popular Music. Indianapolis: Bobbs-Merrill, 1964.
   Covers rock, jazz, folk, country and western music with scattered references to women performers in each category.

479 Dallas, K. "Fine Feathered Folk." Melody Maker 41:22, December 17, 1966.
   This exposition on female folk singers includes photographs.

480 _____. "Pop Is So Male-Oriented--They Don't Think a Lady Can Tell Them Anything." Melody Maker 45:27, August 8, 1970.

481 Dalton, David. Janis. New York: Simon and Schuster, 1971.
   Includes information about Janis Joplin along with photographs. Songs she has written are included.

482 Dalton, M. A. "WBDNA Summer Meeting." School Musician 47:62-63, August-September 1975.
   Concerns the Women Band Directors National Association.

483 Dawbarn, B. "The Birds Is Coming!" Melody Maker 39:3, October 24, 1964.
   Female vocalists are discussed.

484 De Bidoli, Emi. Reminiscences of a Vocal Teacher. Ann Arbor, Mich.: Edwards Brothers, 1946.

485 "Defining Their Role." Opera News 40:16-19, February 14, 1976.
   A symposium on defining the role of women in the arts.

486 De LaGrange, Henry-Louis. "Nadia Boulanger, a Teacher Who Has Inspired Many American Composers." Musical America 76:15, February 15, 1956.
   Miss Boulanger of France has had a great influence on American music especially through her

teaching of composition and piano. Some of her most famous pupils are Aaron Copland, Roy Harris, and Virgil Thomson.

487 De Lorenzo, Leonard. "Some Notes about Women Flutists and Correspondence with G. B. S." Woodwind World 2:7-8, September 1958.
  Although women still face difficulties becoming members of orchestras in the 1950's, women flutists were numerous at the time of Alexander the Great.

488 Denisoff, R. Serge. Sing a Song of Social Significance. Bowling Green, Ohio: Bowling Green University Popular Press, 1972.
  Songs of persuasion, songs of the counter culture, and protest songs (as those sung by Joan Baez) are explored.

489 Dennis, Charles M. "California Parent-Teacher Association Mothersingers." Music Educators Journal 4:45, November-December 1954.
  Seven hundred women made up this choir of "Mothersingers" in their 1954 concert. This group was comprised of P.T.A. members from the Los Angeles City Schools and has been in existence since 1930.

490 Derhen, Andrew. "MOMA: Women Composers; Summergarden Concert." High Fidelity/Musical America 25:MA27-28, December 1975.
  This League of Women Composers is attempting to have women's compositions heard more often. A performance promoting women's works was given in the Summergarden of New York's Museum of Modern Art in August. The different works on the program were reviewed, and the conclusion was that "women can compose just as well--or just as poorly--as men."

491 _____. "Mostly Mozart Festival." High Fidelity/ Musical America 25:MA23, November 1975.
  Antonia Brico recently conducted a concert in the "Mostly Mozart Festival" in New York. She is seventy-three and it has been thirty years since she appeared professionally.

492 De Schauensee, Max. "Stars before Stella." Opera News 22:8, March 14, 1958.

The role of Cio-Cio-San in Puccini's Madame Butterfly was most successfully sung by Geraldine Farrar according to this critic. Other singers who have performed in this role are compared with her.

493 De Toledano, Ralph. "Perennial Ella." National Review 10:194, March 25, 1961.
A critique of the talent of Ella Fitzgerald the Negro singer.

494 De Turk, David A., and Poulin, A. The American Folk Scene; Dimensions of the Folksong Revival. New York: Dell Pub. Co., 1967.
An examination of folk music by many music critics. Two sections are devoted to the folk music of Joan Baez.

495 Detzer, K. "Song Along the Wabash." Recreation 33:663-664, March 1940.
"Farm women's choruses are spreading east and west from Indiana."

496 "A Digest of Mrs. Miller's Report on 'The Parade of American Music.'" Music Clubs Magazine 34:28, June 1955.

497 "Dionne Warwick Ghetto Work Reflects New Mood of Negro Show Bizites." Variety 251:1, July 17, 1968.

498 Discus. "Two Great Women Pianists." Harper's Magazine 228:109-110, January 1964.
Guiomar Novaes first performed in America in 1915 and Gina Bachauer in 1950. Some earlier women keyboard artists are also mentioned. Critiques of some of their recordings are included.

499 "Diskers Yen Sister Chicks Who Can Chirp." Variety 198:1, March 9, 1955.

500 "Doing the Undoable." Time 88:95, December 9, 1966.
Sarah Caldwell conducted the Boston Opera Company in the first U.S. performance of Moses and Aaron. Schoenberg, the composer, felt it was "undoable" since it calls for demanding musical expertise as well as "an orgy of sexual excesses." Ms. Caldwell's successful production of this work shows the Boston Opera Company is an innovative one.

501 Drinker, Sophie Lewis. "What Price Women's Chorus?" Music Journal 12:19, January 1954.
   A chorus for women often fulfills a need that is not met by a conventional mixed chorus. Unfortunately, there is a lack in both quality and quantity of music available for this medium in Drinker's opinion.

502 Duston, A. "19-Store Owner Lauds Women." Billboard 84:1, September 2, 1972.
   The Record Shop, a chain of stores in six states, is unique in that each shop has a woman manager. The president of the chain is quite satisfied with their work.

503 Dutton, William S. "Why Not Music Like This in All Hospitals?" Reader's Digest 68:197, January 1956.
   Gray ladies at Philadelphia's General Hospital are making music in the wards to heal bodies and souls.

504 Dyer, R. "Music; Caldwell's Production of Prokofiev's War and Peace." Nation 218:668-670, May 25, 1974.

505 Dyler, W. "Letters: Composing Women." High Fidelity/Musical America 23:8, May 1973.
   Letters to the editor augmenting a previous list of women composers and giving additional reasons for the failure of women to become great composers.

506 Eaton, Quaintance. "Women Come into Their Own in Our Orchestras." Musical America 75:30, February 15, 1955.
   There are fewer orchestras composed entirely of women during 1955 than in the past, but more women are being admitted into previously all-male orchestras. The statistics are that female members currently comprise 18.4 per cent of the major symphony orchestras.

507 _____. "Women Composers Honored." Music Clubs Magazine 48:42, 1969.

508 Eberhart, Jonathan. "Physics for the Queen." Science News 91:212-213, March 4, 1967.
   Mrs. Carleen Maley Hutchins of New Jersey has designed a family of eight stringed instruments (compared to the usual four: violin, viola, cello, and bass viol). She arrived at this "ideal" group of musical instruments through her work in acoustical theory.

509 Edwards, J. S. "The Centerpiece--or, Who Gets the Flowers?" American Symphony Orchestra League Newsletter 15:23-25, July-September 1964.
   Opinions on the sometimes difficult relationship between the symphony orchestra managers and the women's associations.

510 "Elaine Lorillard Seeks East-West Jazz Swap." Down Beat 33:11, June 30, 1966.
   Mrs. Lorillard represents the Citizens Exchange Corps. She was planning to travel to the U.S.S.R. to propose that the two countries widen their exchanges of musicians to include jazz performers.

511 Eldred, Patricia Mulrooney. Diana Ross. Mankato, Minn.: Creative Education, 1975.
   The biography of this singer's career beginning with the Supremes and Motown Records. For juveniles.

512 "Ella Fitzgerald, Others Win $7,500 Settlement from Pan Am on Bias Rap." Variety 205:41, January 23, 1957.
   Discrimination of black musicians is noted.

513 "Ella, Oscar Peterson Star as 'JATP' Tour Begins." Down Beat 18:1, December 28, 1951.
   Ella Fitzgerald is one of the principal performers in the "Jazz at the Philharmonic" series.

514 "Ella Steals the Show at JATP debut." Melody Maker 28:1, April 5, 1952.
   A review of Ella Fitzgerald in concert in the program "Jazz at the Philharmonic."

515 Ellington, Edward Kennedy. Music Is My Mistress. New York: Da Capo Press, 1976.
   Duke Ellington's story which includes memories of his friends Lena Horne and Ella Fitzgerald.

516 Elson, James. "Practical Aspects of Our Art; Music Selection and Program Building for the Women's Chorus." Choral Journal 13:18-19, October 1972.
   Suggestions for the selection of works for a women's choir director. Bibliographies are listed which can assist in the selection process.

517 English, M. "Luvs Story; Girls' Band." Look 31:M14, May 2, 1967.

518 English, Mary E. "Creative Programming for Women's Choral Ensembles." Choral Journal 6:10-11, 1966.
Includes a list of music.

519 _____. "Women's Choirs in Higher Education." Music Educators Journal 46:62-64, November-December 1959.
Answers are given to the question, "Why have women's choirs?"

520 "Entertaining Diahann Carroll." Harper's Bazaar 102:236-237, November 1968.

521 Epstein, M. "Americans in America." Opera News 39:12-15, March 8, 1975.
Opera singers who are native Americans singing in the U.S. are discussed.

522 Erhardt-Snyder, William. "Prima Donna's Pranks." Etude 5:667, October 1939.
There are references in music literature about the temperamental behavior of women opera stars. Some incidents are related.

523 Esquire's World of Jazz. New York: Thomas Y. Crowell Co., 1975.
Part 4 "Women in Jazz" describes the rise of women jazz musicians and discusses individuals who have succeeded. Among them are Bessie Smith, Ella Fitzgerald, and Billie Holiday.

524 Ewen, David. Men and Women Who Make Music. New York: Readers Press, 1945.
Includes four women musicians: Marian Anderson, Lotte Lehman, Grace Moore, and Lily Pons.

525 "Exhibition: Contemporary Women Composers in the United States." Musical America 83:12, August 1963.
The New York Public Library Music Division had an exhibition on display to commemorate ten American women composers. Among them were Miriam Gideon, Mary Howe, and Louise Talma.

526 "Fancy Wrappings and Sweet Music for Diahann." Life

52:111, April 27, 1962.
   Diahann Carroll has been starring in the Broadway musical No Strings. Her wardrobe and vocal talents have been receiving good reviews.

527 "Fanny Fly Back to U. K. for European Tour." Melody Maker 47:55, September 30, 1972.
   The all-female rock group Fanny continues touring and proving that women can produce popular rock music.

528 "Farewell, Marian Anderson." Ebony 20:39, June 1965.
   Marian Anderson the famous Negro contralto gives a farewell concert tour.

529 Fariña, Richard. "Baez & Dylan; A Generation Sings Out." Mademoiselle 59:242, August 1964.
   An examination of the protest songs that have become a large part of the folk songs being sung by Joan Baez and Bob Dylan.

530 Farnsworth, Paul R. "The Effects of Role-Taking on Artistic Achievement." Journal of Aesthetics and Art Criticism 18(3); 345-349, 1960.
   Vocal music appears to be the only area in music where women have excelled. The conclusion is that women have not felt accepted in the other areas of music which are dominated by men, and therefore, have not tried to enter those fields.

531 Favis-Artsay, A. "Thelma Votipka Featured on LP: American Lady Singers." Hobbies 71:36, February 1967.

532 "Favorite All-Around Female Vocalist." Billboard 61: 30, October 22, 1949 Suppl.

533 Feather, Leonard. "Barbara Carroll Bopped Early." Down Beat 18:2, October 19, 1951.
   Barbara Carroll is possibly the only girl to play bop piano professionally in New York during 1951. She led a trio, but preferred working alone. When asked her ambition Carroll replied, "I want to get married."

534 _____. "Beryl Best Since Mary Lou?" Down Beat 19:8, April 4, 1952.

Beryl Brooker is possibly the most talented jazz piano player since Mary Lou Williams. Brooker tells how she started playing in the Philadelphia bars and became part of several groups.

535 _____. Inside Be-bop. New York: J. J. Robbins, 1949.
A brief history of that aspect of jazz known as bebop beginning about 1940. Information on the principal bands that played this style of music is presented. A few women are included such as the singer Sarah Vaughan and the pianist Barbara Carroll.

536 _____. "This Chick Plays like Navarro." Down Beat 18:3, April 6, 1951.
Norma Carson is a trumpet player who wants the opportunity to play with good jazz bands. Her experiences with all-female groups have not been very successful because "... there are never enough good girl musicians at any one time in any one place to make a good band."

537 _____ and Tracy, Jack. Laughter from the Hip. New York: Horizon Press, 1963.
Reminiscences of famous jazzmen. Few references are made to women, but the most prominent ones such as Billie Holiday are mentioned.

538 Fellows, Myles. "Here Is Mary Garden." Etude 70: 14, April 1952.
The story of this Scottish singer who grew up in the United States. This interview gives some of her opinions and advice on selecting a good vocal teacher.

539 "Female Artists Spur Gains Made by Country Market." Billboard 83:44, February 6, 1971.
Women are doing better in the country music charts than at any time previously, according to the 1971 report. This trend toward hits is demonstrated by the success of Lynn Anderson's "Rose Garden."

540 "Female Deejay." Billboard 61:20, January 15, 1949.
Carol Reed of Philadelphia's station WPTZ became the first female disk jockey on television.

541 "Female Hall of Fame." Jazz Forum 6(17):46-53, 1972.
Includes portraits of women in jazz.

542 "Female Rock." Time 97:68, April 12, 1971.
   There are few female rock groups on the scene, but some notable ones are developing partially because of the women's liberation movement. Four groups are reviewed: Pride of Women, Goldflower, Fanny, and Joy of Cooking (owned and led by two women backed up by three men).

543 "Femme Chirpers Coming into Their Own As Headliners of Television." Variety 189:1, January 21, 1953.

544 "Femme Singers Glutting Market; Even Standouts Can't Find Cafe Bookings." Variety 274:1, April 10, 1974.

545 "Femmes Fostered Opera in US, Sez Mary Garden; Pix, Radio, TV Killed It." Variety 176:2, October 12, 1949.

546 Ferguson, Charles W. "Dorothy Maynor." PTA Magazine 64:10-12, November 1969.
   Maynor is considered an "unexcelled concert singer" according to Ferguson. She might have become a famous opera singer except for the fact that Negroes were not accepted on the opera stage during the peak of her career.

547 Ferrier, Winifred. The Life of Kathleen Ferrier. London: Readers Union, 1955.
   A biography of this English singer by her sister. Includes information about her American tour in 1949.

548 "Few Chick Hits but Fem Titles Burgeon." Billboard 70:40, January 20, 1958.
   There are few hits written by women in rock and roll music during 1958, but there are many about the subject of women. Some examples are the Everly Brothers' "Wake Up Little Susie," the Playmates' "Jo Ann," and Paul Anka's "Diana."

549 "Finn's Jennies." Time 45:58, April 9, 1945.
   "A choir of 80 nuns sang on a public stage for the first time in history." Father William J. Finn is their director; his group has been dubbed "Finn's Jennies."

550 "First Lady." Newsweek 85:77, April 1975.
   Sarah Caldwell is the first woman conductor to

direct the Metropolitan Opera. She has a long record of success in opera production, chiefly at the Boston Opera Company.

551 "First Women's Band of the Marines; New Organization at Camp Lejeune." Musician 50:56-57, March 1945.
Pictures and information on the new all-woman Marine band at Camp Lejeune, North Carolina.

552 Fishel, Elizabeth. "Holly Near: Putting Politics to Music." Ms. 5:31, October 1976.
Holly Near is a feminist singer and songwriter who is involved in various political issues. This interview examines her philosophies and her career.

553 Fisher, Renee B. Musical Prodigies; Master at an Early Age. New York: Association Press, 1973.
Among the girls, prodigy vocalists listed include Ella Fitzgerald, Billie Holiday, and Aretha Franklin.

554 Fitzgerald, Gerald. Callas; The Art and the Life. New York: Holt, Rinehart and Winston, 1974.
The story of Maria Callas and her career in opera. Photographs from her many performances appear on almost every page.

555 _____. "Heroine at Home." Opera News 25:14-15, February 4, 1961.
Leontyne Price is discussed.

556 Fitzlyon, April. The Price of Genius: A Life of Pauline Viardot. New York: Appleton-Century, 1964.
Pauline Viardot-García (her married name which she used professionally) was a talented operatic performer and teacher. Among her most famous students was Beverly Sills.

557 "Folk-Girls." Time 79:39-40, June 1, 1962.
"Current wave of young girl folk singers is led by Joan Baez who scorns commercial success. Others are Bonnie Dobson, Judy Collins, and Juliette Hester."

558 "Former Supreme Talks a Little." Ebony 24:83, February 1969.
Florence Ballard tells why she quit (or was asked to leave) the Supremes, an extremely successful singing trio. No conclusive answer is given, but she discusses the group's success story.

559 Forsee, Aylesa. <u>American Women Who Scored Firsts</u>. Philadelphia: Macrae Smith Co., 1958.
    Among the various biographical sketches of great American women is Marian Anderson who made great progress for Negroes in the music field.

560 Forster, P. "Caricatures." <u>About the House</u> 4(10):60-61, 1975.
    Consists of caricatures of famous sopranos in typical roles.

561 "Four Girls." <u>Newsweek</u> 43:80, June 28, 1954.
    A woman's quartet that sings gospel songs was composed of Hollywood Christians. The actresses Jane Russell and Rhonda Fleming were two of the members who recorded religious songs.

562 Fowler, Charles B. "On Education." <u>High Fidelity/Musical America</u> 26:MA8-9, December 1976.
    This article discusses the problem of sex discrimination in an all-boy choir in Wethersfield, Connecticut. This is a violation of the government's sex bias law in the view of some. Fowler's conclusion is that "sex bias is a legitimate concern, but the focus of it is hardly the music classroom."

563 Frame, Florence K. "Women Can Play in Orchestras." <u>Music Journal</u> 16:66, March 1958.
    Although many symphony orchestras have accepted women, it is still difficult for women to obtain positions in this field. Mrs. Margaret Foote, concert master of Colorado Springs Symphony Orchestra, urged talented girls to pursue this career since things are changing in favor of women.

564 Frank, Gerold. <u>Judy</u>. New York: Harper & Row, 1975.
    This is the authorized biography of Judy Garland. It is an extensive work about her life.

565 "Fraternity Composers Honored." <u>Pan Pipes</u> 62:40, January 1970.
    The Musicians Club of New York recently performed a Concert of Chamber Music Works by American Women Composers. Louise Talma was one of those composers included.

566 Frederick, R. "Economics of the Modern Soprano."
Variety 239:56, July 7, 1965.

567 Freedland, Nat. "Distaffers Dominating Pop Charts.
Billboard 85:1, April 7, 1973.
Women popular music singers are dominating record sales in 1973 more than at any time since the early 1960's. Carly Simon, Helen Reddy, and Roberta Flack are the big sellers.

568 _____. "Fems Say Chauvinism Prevails in Industry."
Billboard 86:1, November 30, 1974.
Hiring practices in the music field still favor men, women charge. When Billboard announced it was seeking input on this subject, a large number of women offered their histories of repression in the music industry. Some of these cases are cited.

569 Freeman, John W. "Whose Little Girl Are You?"
Opera News 32:6-7, March 2, 1968.
Discussion of "matronly" girls of opera. Dramatic sopranos often perform the roles of young sylphlike maidens, but seldom look the part.

570 Fretwell, Dorrie S. "Let the Ladies Do It." High Fidelity/Musical America 25:MA14-16, September 1975.
Women's organizations are a major force in raising funds for the various symphony orchestras in the nation. Details are given about individual groups.

571 Friedman, Myra. Buried Alive; The Biography of Janis Joplin. New York: William Morrow, 1973.
The biography of this hard rock and blues singer's life.

572 Fudger, M. "Rock Giants from A-Z; Janis Joplin: Martyr to Her Music." Melody Maker 49:21-22, January 5, 1974.

573 Gahr, David, and Shelton, Robert. The Face of Folk Music. New York: Citadel Press, 1968.
A book of photographs of folk singers from all over the world. Most are Americans. Among them are many women, including Joan Baez, Joni Mitchell, and Aretha Franklin.

574 "Gal Singer-Writers Swell ASCAP, BMI Membership Rolls." Variety 268:47, November 8, 1972.

575 "Gal Vocalists Dropping Orchs for Solo Stints on Disks, TV." Variety 183:41, August 29, 1951.

576 Galatopoulos, Stelios. Callas: La Divina; Art That Conceals Art. Rev. ed. London: Dent, 1966.
　　The biography of Maria Callas who was born in New York. Included is an analysis of the most famous roles she has performed in opera.

577 "Gals from the Hills; Kitty and Goldie Start Country-Girl Search." Billboard 65:1, June 20, 1953.
　　There has been a concentrated effort to locate female country singers ever since Kitty Wells made a hit with the song "It Wasn't God Who Made Honky Tonk Angels" and Goldie Hill recorded "I Let the Stars Get in My Eyes." Recording experts note that these two hits have promoted enthusiasm for women country music singers.

578 "Gals 'Taking Over' in Rock 'n' Roll As Femme Instrumentalists Soar." Variety 257:49, November 19, 1969.
　　A current list of women in rock music; none of these have replaced the well-known singers Grace Slick and Janis Joplin.

579 Gardner, Mark. "Sarah Vaughan Bargains." Jazz Journal 20:8-10, January 1967.
　　The buyer is alerted to be careful of cheap label discography. Vaughan's singing is evaluated on several of her records.

580 Garland, Phyl. "Nina Simone, High Priestess of Soul." Ebony 24:156-159, August 1969.
　　An excerpt from The Sound of Soul--The Music and Its Meaning.

581 _____. "Roberta Flack: New Musical Messenger." Ebony 26:54, January 1971.
　　Roberta Flack was a school teacher in Washington, D.C., before she became a singing success in rock music.

582 _____. The Sound of Soul--the Music and Its Meaning. Chicago: H. Regnery, 1969.

Two chapters emphasize women singers: "Nina Simone: High Priestess of Soul" and "Aretha Franklin: Sister Soul."

583 Gehrkens, Karl W. "Can a College Girl Major in Music?" Etude 70:23, March 1952.
Advice to a woman student on the usual courses of study involved in a music major and on how to select a good school.

584 _____. "Can a Woman Conduct an Orchestra?" Etude 61:168, March 1943.
There has been a history of men as symphony performers and conductors, but Gehrkens believes this will change in the future.

585 Gelatt, Roland. Music Makers; Some Outstanding Musical Performers of Our Day. New York: Knopf, 1953.
Twenty-one musicians are discussed in this book, four of them women. None is an American. However, their concerts in the United States were important in the musical development of this country. Myra Hess is one of those discussed.

586 _____. "Music: The Met's Top Three Sopranos." Reporter 15:39-40, November 29, 1956.

587 Gerhardt, Elena. Recital. London: Methuen, 1953.
Elena Gerhardt's autobiography. This German singer shares her experiences of concert life in America.

588 Gerke, Madge Cathcart. "Mu Phi Epsilon Women in American Symphony Orchestras." Triangle 69(4):7-8, 1975.
A listing of women symphony members in Mu Phi Epsilon orchestras by state.

589 "Girl Lechers Who Follow Musicians: Theme of 'Rock 70.'" Variety 255:2, July 23, 1969.

590 "Girl Shortage Alarms Music Biz." Melody Maker 35:1, November 12, 1960.

591 "Girl Singers in Disk Vogue Again with Hits in Pop, Jazz & Folk." Variety 232:59, September 18, 1963.

592 "Girl Vocalists." Metronome 74:26-29, January 1957.
Recordings of popular singers are discussed.

593 "The Girls." BMI October 1969, pp. 12-13.
Discussion of Hubert Saal's article in Newsweek, July 14, 1969, in which he comments on women musicians who write and sing their own songs. Among these musicians are Joni Mitchell and Lotti Golden.

594 "Girls from Motown; The Supremes." Time 87:83-84, March 4, 1966.
The Supremes made their first money singing in a ghetto backyard in Detroit. Since then this trio of girls have been earning $5,000 per performance in such exclusive places as Manhattan's Copacabana.

595 "Girls, Girls, Girls." Melody Maker 41:17, February 19, 1966.
Girls who sing popular music are discussed.

596 "Girls, Girls, Girls--They're Putting Their Best Foot Forward." Billboard 83:32, October 16, 1971 Suppl.

597 Gitler, Ira. Jazz Masters of the Forties. New York: Macmillan Co., 1966.
Sarah Vaughan is the most prominent woman in this history of jazz musicians of the 1940's.

598 "Glamor Gallery." Theatre Arts 37:78-79, December 1953.
"Replacing the portly singers of yesteryear, the Met's modern divas appeal to the eye as well as the ear." Lily Pons and Risë Stevens are two of the singers mentioned.

599 Glenn, C. "In Quest of Answers: Women Conductors." Choral Journal 16(4):24-25, 1975.
Choral directors share their opinions about women conductors.

600 "Gold Baton Award Certificates Presented to Symphony Women's Association Representatives at League Banquet." American Symphony Orchestra League Newsletter 13(5):5, 1962.
A list of the associations and their representatives who received these awards at the 1962 convention banquet.

601 Goldman, Albert. "Drugs and Death in the Run-Down World of Rock Music." Life 69:32-33, October 16, 1970.
 Janis Joplin is discussed in this article on rock musicians who have died from drugs.

602 _____. "Return of the Queen of Shebang." Life 69:11, October 2, 1970.
 Nina Simone, a black woman who studied at New York's Juilliard School of Music, has discovered that singing jazz in the style of Billie Holiday has been more profitable than using her conservatory training.

603 _____. "A Season Saved by the Belles." Life 71:R, December 31, 1971.
 An article reviewing the important role women have played in writing popular songs.

604 Goldreich, Gloria, and Goldreich, Ester. What Can She Be?: A Musician. New York: Lothrop, Lee and Shepard, 1975.
 Music as a profession for women is examined in this book designed for young people.

605 Goldstein, R. "Ladies' Day; Janis Joplin ... Staggering." Vogue 151:164, May 1968.
 Janis Joplin was possibly the leading woman in rock music although others like Cass Elliot of the Mamas and the Papas and Grace Slick of the Jefferson Airplane have had an impact. Joplin's blues renditions were often similar to the style of Bessie Smith.

606 Goldstein, Toby. "A Reviewer Reviews Reviewers' Views of Women's Bands: From between the Sheets." Modern Hi Fi and Stereo Guide November 1974, pp. 41-46.

607 Goreau, Laurraine. Just Mahalia, Baby. Waco, Texas: Word Books, 1975.
 An extensive biography of Mahalia Jackson's life as a gospel singer.

608 Gould, Glenn. "The Search for Petula Clark." High Fidelity/Musical America 17:67-71, November 1967.
 The story of this popular singer's career.

609 Grafman, Howard, and Manning, B. T. Folk Music U.S.A. New York: Citadel Press, 1962.
   The major portion of this book consists of photographs and biographical sketches of American folk singers. Among them are many women such as Mahalia Jackson, Barbara Dane, and Jean Ritchie.

610 "Grandmas' Ragtime Band." American Magazine 149: 116, May 1950.

611 Gravina, Peter. "Artists in the Kitchen." Opera News 30:26-29, March 19, 1966.
   A number of opera singers are gourmet cooks at home and on tour. Some of their recipes are given.

612 Gray, Michael. "The Sex Bar." Melody Maker 49:51, June 8, 1974.

613 _____. "Sexist Songs." Melody Maker 49:18-19, June 1, 1974.

614 _____. "Women and Rock." Melody Maker 49:36-37, May 25, 1974.

615 Gray, N. J. "Women in Music Education." School Musician 47:54-55, December 1975.

616 Green, Benny. The Reluctant Art; The Growth of Jazz. New York: Horizon Press, 1963.
   One of the six chapters in this work treats Billie Holiday and her influence on jazz.

617 Green, M. S. "Women: From Silence to Song." NATS Bulletin 32(2):25-27, 1975.

618 Greenbie, S. "Melody from the Distaff." Saturday Review 31:30, April 24, 1948.
   A review of Sophie Lewis Drinker's book Music and Women: The Story of Women in Their Relation to Music.

619 Greene, Richard L. "Male Oppression of Women Composers." Saturday Review 55:6, January 8, 1972.
   This writer suggests that both male and female concert patrons should protest the all-male composed programs that are offered year after year. He suggests writing congressmen and concert managers to try to rectify this situation.

620 Greenfield, Edward. Joan Sutherland. New York: Drake Publishers, 1973.
A biography of this famous opera singer's career. She has performed in many operas in the U. S.

621 Grevatt, R. "Gal Singers Make the 'Sick' Scene." Billboard Music Week 73:5, February 27, 1961.

622 _____. "The Girls Are Moving In." Melody Maker 36:9, December 16, 1961.

623 _____. "They're Making Their Move to Take Over Hot 100 Chart." Billboard 75:3, December 7, 1963.

624 Grimes, Sally. "True Death of Bessie Smith." Esquire 71:112-113, June 1969.
Varying accounts of this blues singer's car accident and death are given. Edward Albee is attributed to immortalizing her career by producing his off-Broadway play, The Death of Bessie Smith, in 1961.

625 Groia, Philip. They All Sang on the Corner; New York City Rhythm and Blues Vocal Groups of the 1950's. Rev. ed. Setauket, N. Y.: Edmond Pub. Co., 1974.
A few women are included in this discussion of New York groups of the 1950's.

626 Groom, Bob. The Blues Revival. London: Studio Vista, 1971.
Short references to women are included in this story of the blues.

627 Grunfeld, Frederic V. "Men, Women and Music." Reader's Digest 87:35-36, November 1965.
A humorous essay on the differences in musical taste between the sexes, and the way women have manipulated men and their music through the ages.

628 "Guide for American Composers Radio Series." Music Clubs Magazine 51(5):12-14, 1972.

629 Haines, Connie. For Once in My Life. New York: Warner Books, 1976.
The story of Connie Haines and her career in music.

630 Haley, Alex. "She Makes a Joyful Music." Reader's Digest 79:196-198, November 1961.

Mahalia Jackson is one of the world's foremost gospel singers. She was uncomfortable singing other types of songs. There was hope in singing the Lord's music, she felt.

631 Hamblin, Dora Jane. "She Puts Oomph in the Opera." Life 58:77-78, March 5, 1965.
Sarah Caldwell is deeply involved in operatic productions of the Boston Opera Company as conductor and stage director. A documented story of her problems and joys in working with this group is given.

632 Hamilton, J. "Supremes; From Real Rags to Real Riches." Look 30:70, May 3, 1966.

633 Hammond, J. "Symphony of the New World." Instrumental Musician 67:11, August 1968.

634 Handly, Donna. "Yes, Virginia. There Are Women Composers and Conductors." Ms. 3:19, August 1974.
The Cabrillo Music Festival to be held in Aptos, California, will feature works exclusively by women composers.

635 Hansen, Barry. "Barbara Dane Sings the Blues." Sing Out 14:19-22, April-May 1964.
There was a time when only black women sang blues, but this is no longer true. Barbara Dane is one of these blues singers currently performing around the nation.

636 Hardester, Jane S. "Women in Choral Music." Choral Journal 15(1):15-16, 1974.
In this paper, which was first presented at a MENC meeting, Ms. Hardester recounts the discrimination women have suffered in all aspects of society. Choral music was not specifically discussed.

637 Harman, Carter. "Pappy, Listen to Petula; The Bittersweet Voice of Petula Clark." Life 59:23, December 10, 1965.
Petula Clark is a rock singer who has become popular with her sweet, understandable songs among both the young and the old.

638 Harris, Kenn. Renata Tebaldi. New York: Drake Publishers, 1974.

The soprano's career at the Metropolitan Opera, beginning in 1954 through the 1970's, is explored.

639 Harris, M. "Woman in the Pit; Composer-Conductor." Newsweek 80:82-83, August 21, 1972.
Margaret Harris is a 28-year-old black woman who conducted over 800 performances of Hair in New York in 1972. In addition to conducting, she composes songs.

640 "Harry and Lena Off the Cuff!" Ebony 25:128-129, March 1970.
Lena Horne is interviewed.

641 Harwood, R. P. "Mighty Tight Woman; The Thomas Family and Classic Blues." Storyville 17:16-25, June-July 1968.

642 Havener, H. "Girl with a Baton." Independent Woman 27:328-330, November 1948.

643 Hawkins, M. "Women at the Console." Musical Opinion 77:495, May 1954.
Women organists are discussed.

644 Hawkins, Mrs. Robert. "Our Fair Ladies (Women Band Directors)." School Musician 41:58-59, November 1969.
A compilation of women band directors' feelings about working in this previously all-male field, along with advice for future female band directors.

645 _____. "Yes, I'm the Band Director's Wife." School Musician 24:10, November 1952.

646 Hayes, C. J. "Mahalia Jackson, a Discography." Matrix 62:3-5, December 1965.

647 Hays, William. Twentieth-Century Views of Music History. New York: Charles Scribner's Sons, 1972.
In Chapter 32 on "Jazz As Folk and Art Music" black women such as Bessie Smith, Mahalia Jackson, and Marian Anderson are discussed.

648 Hebson, Ann. "Women Can Become Successful University Music Professors." School Musician 40:52-53, January 1969.

Interviews with two women professors in low brass at the University of Miami at Coral Gables, Fla.: Dorothy Ziegler and Constance Weldon.

649 Heilbut, Tony. <u>The Gospel Sound; Good News and Bad Times.</u> New York: Simon & Schuster, 1971.
Black women have played a significant role in the history of American gospel music. This book contains much information on the great names as well as lesser-known singers. Sallie Martin, Mahalia Jackson, and Bessie Griffin each have a chapter devoted to them.

650 Helm, MacKinley. <u>Angel Mo' and Her Son, Roland Hayes.</u> Boston: Little, Brown and Co., 1944.
The biography of the black singer Roland Hayes focusing on his mother's influence.

651 Helman, H. "The Organists' and Choralists' Round Table." <u>Music Teacher and Piano Student</u> 32:199, April 1953.
Includes a list of new choral works for women's choirs.

652 Hemming, Roy. "Lively Arts." <u>Senior Scholastic</u> 94: 21-22, May 2, 1969.
Betty Allen a black mezzo-soprano is interviewed. She reveals some of the difficulties she has faced in finding American jobs especially at the Metropolitan Opera.

653 _____. "Peggy Lee." <u>Senior Scholastic</u> 97:19, October 5, 1970.
An interview with Peggy Lee who has been a popular music singer during the past twenty years.

654 Henahan, D. "Prodigious Sarah." <u>New York Times Magazine</u> October 5, 1975, p. 20.
Discussion of the prominent conductor Sarah Caldwell.

655 Henderson, William James. "Female Song Birds Duly Noted." <u>American Record Guide</u> 25:569, May 1959.
Includes the greatest women singers at the Metropolitan Opera House in New York.

656 Henshaw, L. "Aretha, the Girl Who Draws Pictures When She Sings." <u>Melody Maker</u> 43:7, September 7, 1968.

Aretha Franklin's style of singing is critiqued.

657 Hentoff, Nat. "Cherchez les Femmes." Down Beat 19:5, December 3, 1952.
Hentoff cites examples of discrimination against women in various aspects of the music industry. He is optimistic that this situation will change in the near future.

658 _____. "Soundings." Jazz & Pop 10:12, June 1971.
An examination of the place of women in rock music.

659 _____. "The Vanishing Female Jazz-Singer." Saturday Review 39:32-33, March 17, 1956.
No women since the 1940's have matched the caliber of jazz music such as that of Bessie Smith and Billie Holiday. Hentoff discusses some of the styles and qualities of singers of the 1950's.

660 Heylbut, Rose. "Prima Donna's Amazing Fight Back to Health and Success: Faith and Music Can Work Miracles." Etude 61:149, March 1943.
Marjorie Lawrence, the Australian soprano who sang with the Metropolitan Opera Company, tells of her struggle to regain her health after a bout with paralysis.

661 _____. "What Music Means to Helen Keller." Etude 60:7, January 1942.
Helen Keller, who became deaf and dumb before she was two, described how she enjoyed music, which she sensed as vibrations.

662 _____. "The Young Career." Etude 70:12, February 1952.
The singer Barbara Gibson tells how one should attempt to begin a musical career.

663 Hill, Roy. "Fannie Douglass Reminiscences of Yesteryear." Black Perspectives in Music 2:54-62, Spring 1974.
An interview with Fannie Howard Douglass who recalls black musicians she has known through the years. For example, she heard Marian Anderson give her first concert at age eighteen in a local high school.

664 Hinton, Sam. "Bess Hawes." Sing Out 15:26-30, September 1965.
   This versatile lady combines careers as folk singer, college teacher, guitar instructor, and wife and mother. The article emphasizes her training and performance in folk music.

665 Holiday, Billie, and Dufty, William. Lady Sings the Blues. Garden City, N.Y.: Doubleday, 1956.
   The autobiography of Billie Holiday.

666 Holly, Hal. "Addition to 'Girls in Jazz' Found on Coast by Holly." Down Beat 18:8, June 15, 1951.

667 _____. "Hormel Conductor Denies Gal Musicians Lack S.A." Down Beat 18:8, June 1, 1951.
   Al Woodbury conducted the Hormel Orchestra which consisted of sixty women instrumentalists in 1951. He disagreed with Lorraine (Mrs. Xavier) Cugat's statements that a woman cannot be glamorous and play a wind instrument at the same time.

668 _____. "Mrs. Cugat Can't See Gals As Tooters; Kills Glamor." Down Beat 18:13, May 4, 1951.
   Lorraine Cugat, a band leader, will hire only men for her Latin-American band. She asserts that "only men ... can play that music with the required fire."

669 "Hooray for the Yé-Yé Girls." Life 56:39, May 29, 1964.

670 Horne, Lena. "I Just Want to Be Myself." Show 3: 62-65, September 1963.

671 _____; Arstein, Helen; and Moss, Carlton. In Person; Lena Horne. New York: Greenberg, 1950.
   Relates the problems Lena Horne encountered during her career in show business.

672 _____ and Schickel, Richard. Lena. Garden City, N.Y.: Doubleday, 1965.
   The story of Lena Horne's life as a singer and actress with much material about her childhood.

673 Hourigan, Virginia. "A Woman Who Doubles." Woodwind World 12(5):10-11, 1973.
   Ms. Hourigan writes about her career as a wood-

wind expert. She discovered that a bassoonist's repertoire was limited, so she concentrated on the flute, oboe, and clarinet as well. In March of 1973 she performed a concert at Carnegie Hall using all four instruments.

674 Howard, George S. "A Tribute to the Woman Band Director." School Musician 44:76-77, August-September 1972.

Col. Howard discusses several women band directors with whom he has been acquainted and who have done excellent jobs: Mildred Reiner, Leonore Johnson, Ramona Meltz, Patricia Hickerson, and Gladys Wright.

675 Howe, Mark Anthony De Wolfe. The Tale of Tanglewood; Scene of the Berkshire Music Festivals. New York: Vanguard Press, 1946.

Women have played an important part in the establishment of Tanglewood. Mrs. Elizabeth Coolidge, one of the founders, was an accomplished musician herself and made significant contributions.

676 Hughes, Allen. "Rosalie Miller Urges Aspiring Singers to Acquire Well-Founded Preparation." Musical America 72:21, December 15, 1952.

This vocal teacher does not encourage all her pupils to pursue operatic careers, but does believe that it offers the greatest challenge to a singer. Popular music is perfectly acceptable to her from a vocal standpoint as long as it is sung correctly.

677 Hunt, M. "Let's Face It." Woodwind Magazine 1:5, May 1949.

Discussion of discrimination against women in music.

678 Hurok, S. Impresario; A Memoir. New York: Random House, 1946.

Memoirs of this manager's years working with great artists from all over the world including American women such as Marian Anderson.

679 Hush, Michele. "Yoko on Women." Rock February 11, 1974, pp. 12-13.

Yoko Ono discusses women in rock music.

680 "Ike & Tina Turner." Ebony 26:88, May 1971.
    Tina Turner is sometimes referred to as the current "high priestess of rock."

681 Ingram, M. D. "Big Sister Choirs." Journal of Church Music 8:1-10, June 1966.
    Youth choirs are discussed.

682 Irving, Clive. "Against the Odds." McCalls 99:17, November 1971.

683 "Italo Critics Tag Bette Midler Tops." Variety 275:43, July 10, 1974.

684 "It's a Man's World Again on Wax As Crooners Displace Canaries." Variety 192:57, October 7, 1953.

685 Jackson, Jesse. Make a Joyful Noise unto the Lord: The Life of Mahalia Jackson, Queen of Gospel Singers. New York: Thomas Y. Crowell, 1974.
    A biography of the well-known black gospel singer written for the young reader.

686 Jackson, Mahalia, and Wylie, Evan M. Movin' on Up. New York: Hawthorn Books, 1966.
    Story of Mahalia Jackson's career singing her "songs of hope."

687 Jacobs, Linda. Cher: Simply Cher. St. Paul, Minn.: EMC Corp., 1975.
    Biography of Cher Bono. Juvenile literature.

688 _____. Olivia Newton-John, the Sunshine Supergirl. St. Paul, Minn.: EMC Corp., 1975.
    Biography written for young people. This English-born singer became popular in the U.S. before she had visited here.

689 _____. Roberta Flack; Sound of Velvet Melting. St. Paul, Minn.: EMC Corp., 1975.
    Juvenile literature of this black singer.

690 Jacobson, R. "Report: Sarah Caldwell Opens Sixteenth Season with Don Quichotte." Opera News 38:22-23, April 13, 1974.
    Caldwell is beginning her sixteenth year as conductor and director of the Boston Opera Company.

Her opera productions have been known for their individuality.

691 _____. "Viewpoint." Opera News 40:4, February 14, 1976.
Women in the arts are examined.

692 Jasper, Tony. Understanding Pop. London: S.C.M. Press, 1972.
This exploration of popular music includes women in groups such as the Supremes and the Mamas and the Papas.

693 Jefferson, Margo. "Belles of the Ball; Patti LaBelle and the Bluebelles." Newsweek 84:113, October 21, 1974.
A chronicle of this all-girl group's beginnings. "LaBelle has revived and refined what the music trade calls 'girl group' rock."

694 _____. "Crossing the Borders." Newsweek 84:61, September 2, 1974.
Carla Borg Bley is discussed in relation to women's place in music.

695 _____. "Great (Hazel) Scott!" Ms. 3:25, November 1974.
An interview with Hazel Scott.

696 _____. "Stevie's Angel." Newsweek 86:71, July 28, 1975.
Minnie Riperton, a Negro singer, is discussed.

697 Jellinek, George. Callas; Portrait of a Prima Donna. New York: Ziff-Davis Pub. Co., 1960.
A biography of Maria Callas's career in opera as it progressed at the major opera houses of Europe and the United States.

698 Joe, R. "SAC Urges More Women in Hi Fi." Billboard 86:1, November 30, 1974.

699 Johnson, Tom. "Musician of the Month." High Fidelity/Musical America 25:MA4-5, June 1975.
Lucia Dlugoszewski is a composer who uses everyday sounds in her musical material. In a concert given in 1951 she separated the audience from the

performers with a screen so that there were no visual distractions from the sounds such as bouncing balls and breaking glass.

700 _____. "New Music." High Fidelity/Musical America 25:MA12-13, June 1975.
Alison Knowles, a painter, has branched out into "created music." One example of her works was "Make a Salad," which consisted of the sounds of vegetables being chopped into pieces on a chopping block.

701 Johnson, W. D. "For Love--Not Money." Bluegrass Unlimited 9:15-17, August 1974.

702 Jones, Hettie. Big Star Fallin' Mama; Five Women in Black Music. New York: Viking Press, 1974.
Ma Rainey, Bessie Smith, Mahalia Jackson, Billie Holiday, and Aretha Franklin are the five women portrayed in this work.

703 Jones, LeRoi. Black Music. New York: W. Morrow, 1971.
A collection of short articles on black music, chiefly jazz, from Billie Holiday to Dionne Warwick.

704 Jones, R. P. Jazz. New York: Roy Publishers, 1963.
Bessie Smith is the woman whose music was analyzed in the greatest depth in this work.

705 Jorgensen, J. "Marie Knight." Melody Maker 28:9, April 12, 1952.

706 Josephson, M. "Music: Joplin and Hendrix; A Note on the Rhetoric of Death." Art in America 59:96-97, September 1971.
Janis Joplin is discussed.

707 Joslyn, Jay. "Milwaukee Sym." High Fidelity/Musical America 25:MA27, December 1975.
Sarah Caldwell's debut as a conductor of the Milwaukee Symphony Orchestra on September 6 and 7, 1975, is reviewed.

708 "Joyful Noise in Israel." Time 77:81, May 26, 1961.

Mahalia Jackson, a gospel singer, visited Israel and sang there to very responsive audiences.

709 Kahn, D. "Women Build a Symphony." Christian Science Monitor January 4, 1941, p. 5.

710 Kahn, Kath. Hillbilly Women. Garden City, N.Y.: Doubleday, 1973.
Includes information on women country singers.

711 Kalish, E. "Folk Music Plays Big N.Y.B.O. Tune; Weavers, Miss Baez, PP&M Hot 34G." Variety 229:47, November 28, 1962.

712 "Karen Riale Becomes First Woman Member of United States Air Force Band of Washington, D.C." School Music 44:52, June-July 1973.
Sergeant Riale was a clarinetist who was the first woman to perform in one of America's four major military bands.

713 "Kathleen Merritt Orchestra." Musical Opinion 83:599, June 1960.

714 Kefalas, Elinor. "Pauline Oliveros: An Interview." High Fidelity/Musical America 25:MA24-25, June 1975.
Pauline Oliveros is a prominent experimental composer who teaches at the University of California, San Diego. She expresses her views on the role of a woman in composition and the problems she faces.

715 Keller, V. B. "Anniversary Is Noted by Columbus Group." Musical America 76:34, November 1, 1956.
The women's music club of Columbus celebrated its anniversary.

716 Kelly, V. "Diahann Carroll; Show Stopper." Look 26:110, May 22, 1962.
Although she studied piano and voice as preparation for becoming a singer, Diahann Carroll says her real dream was to be the world's best roller skater. In addition to her success in singing she has now added acting on Broadway to her credits.

717 Kemp, Dorothy E. "A Woman Talks Back." Instrumentalist 8:7, May 1954.

A reply to a March 1954 article entitled "Women Are Here to Stay." Ms. Kemp, a college music teacher, shares her experiences of finding many women in all aspects of the music field.

718   Kennedy, P. "Minstrels of the Kentucky Hills; The Traipsin' Woman's Twelfth Annual American Folk Song Festival." Travel 79:14, June 1942.

719   Kennely, P. "Pop Talk." Jazz & Pop 9:48-50, October 1970.
Examination of male dominance in rock and roll.

720   Kettring, Donald D. "Mr. and Mrs. Ministries in Church Music." Journal of Church Music 15:2-6, June 1973.
This article examines the life of the husband-wife team as organist and music director. Kenneth L. Landis and his wife Ellen relate how they cope with this team situation.

721   "Kimball Names First Woman Piano Traveler." Music Trades 119:32, April 1971.

722   "King As Queen?" Time 98:52, July 12, 1971.
Describes Carole King's rise to fame in popular music. Included are three other women in rock music: Carly Simon, Linda Ronstadt, and Rita Coolidge.

723   Kinne, Margaret. "Breathes There a Girl?" Music Journal 16:48, June-July 1958.
Margaret Kinne, a vocal teacher, offers suggestions to improve the tone and breathing of female students. She feels that girls' choirs often look much better than they sound due to improper breathing techniques.

724   Kirby, F. "Gals Air Gripes at NARAS Meet on Women's Role in Music Biz." Variety 277:80, February 5, 1975.

725   Kirsten, Dorothy. "Dorothy Kirsten's Operatic Utopia." Music Journal 22:23, October 1964.
Ms. Kirsten, a noted operatic soprano, has been involved in directing productions in Los Angeles. She

feels that there must be as much realism as possible in productions.

726 Kitt, Eartha. Alone with Me; A New Autobiography. Chicago: H. Regnery Co., 1976.
Autobiography of this singer and actress.

727 _____. Thursday's Child. New York: Duell, Sloan and Pearce, 1956.
The autobiography of this black singer from the South. Her childhood and domestic life are emphasized rather than her career as an entertainer.

728 Kloman, William. "Just Call Us Super Group; The Mamas and the Papas." Saturday Evening Post 240: 36-41, March 25, 1967.
Michelle Phillips and Cass Elliot are the two women in this group of popular singers. Reviews of their singing have been favorable and their records have been selling very well.

729 Knight, Janet. "For the First Time on the Great Stage." Ms. 4:92-93, November 1975.
Photographs and short biographies of five women composers whose works were heard at the New York Philharmonic's "Celebration of Women Composers" November 10, 1976, with Sarah Caldwell as conductor. Profiles of two Americans are included: Ruth Crawford Seeger and Pozzi Escot.

730 "Knowing the Score." Mademoiselle 52:116, November 1960.
Few women have been famous conductors or composers, but two musicians are attempting to change that. Liza Redfield is conducting the musical The Music Man and Emma Lou Diemer is a composer-in-residence in Arlington, Virginia, high schools, where she writes pieces for this age group.

731 Kolodin, Irving. "Great Artists of Our Time." Saturday Review 49:47-49, February 26, 1966.
Birgit Nilsson's many roles at the Metropolitan Opera are reviewed.

732 _____. "Music to My Ears." Saturday Review 48: 32, May 1, 1965.

A review of Marian Anderson's final recital at Carnegie Hall.

733 _____. "Nadia Boulanger." Saturday Review 45:25, March 3, 1962.
This French lady has been teaching composition and piano to Americans such as Aaron Copland since the 1920's.

734 Koopal, Grace G. Miracle of Music; The History of the Hollywood Bowl. Los Angeles: W. Ritchie, 1972.
This is a chronological history of the Hollywood Bowl. Many women have been involved with this outdoor theater in administration as well as musical performances. Mrs. Dorothy Chandler is one who saved it from closing in 1951 because of financial difficulties. At a later date she raised more than $13,000,000 to establish the Music Center in Los Angeles.

735 Korall, G. "ABC's for Aretha." Saturday Review 51: 54-55, March 16, 1968.
A brief description of Aretha Franklin's career and reviews of some of her recorded works.

736 Krehm, Ida. "Why Not Women Conductors?" Music Journal 27:82-83, February 1969.
The prejudice against women conductors is diminishing as other professions have gradually accepted women. Krehm lists some of the women who have managed to conduct orchestras in the past and tells of her own experiences in the field.

737 Kunkel, Marjorie. "Women Can Find Careers in Music." School Musician 45:37, October 1973.
An essay on the positive aspects of a profession in music for women.

738 Kunstadt, L. "Lillyn Brown." Record Research 2:12, November-December 1956.
Lillyn Brown is a blues singer.

739 _____. "Rosa Henderson Sings the Blues; A Race Record Survey." Record Research 3:2, January-February 1958.

740 Kupferberg, Herbert. "America Sings." Atlantic Monthly 220:120-122, September 1967.

The conductor Sarah Caldwell is heading the American National Opera Company, which is partially funded by the government. Her ideas and methods of organizing this touring group are disclosed.

741 _____. Those Fabulous Philadelphians; The Life and Times of a Great Orchestra. New York: C. Scribner's Sons, 1969.
Many women have been orchestra members and soloists through the years in Philadelphia. One section, "Ladies Day," relates the ways Stokowski, the conductor, tried to deal with all the noise which occurred during the Friday afternoon concerts.

742 "The Ladies, Bless 'Em." Musical America 73:21, March 1953.
A letter indicating that the Portland Symphony and Junior Symphony have females in almost every section. Orchestras of the East cannot boast such integration at this time according to this letter in 1953.

743 "Ladies' Day." Time 88:94-95, December 9, 1966.
Women musicians are increasingly being admitted to the orchestras of the U.S. Short case histories of some women are included along with details of problems they encountered in these positions.

744 "Lady Mgr. Using Working Class As Opera Sponsors." Variety 218:73, March 16, 1960.

745 "Lady Soul: Singing It Like It is." Time 91:62-66, June 28, 1968.
Aretha Franklin is the soul singer discussed.

746 "Lady with a Low Flame." Time 99:73-74, June 5, 1972.
The black singer Roberta Flack is interviewed.

747 La Farge, Peter. "Buffy Sainte-Marie." Sing Out 15:34-37, March 1965.
A biographical sketch of this Indian folk singer plus two of her songs.

748 Lage, Wally. "The Women's Army Corps Band." Music Journal Annual 1969, p. 47.
In 1969 Fort McClellan, Alabama, had the only women's band in the armed forces. As in any other

military band, music was the full-time job of these women. Details of their lives as members of a military band were disclosed.

749 Landau, Deborah. Janis Joplin: Her Life and Times. New York: Paperback Library, 1971.
The story of this blues singer's rise to stardom plus pictures and discography. Bessie Smith the black blues singer of an earlier era was one of her idols.

750 Landau, Jon. It's Too Late to Stop Now; A Rock and Roll Journal. San Francisco: Straight Arrow Books, 1972.
This music critic has compiled his memories of rock personalities. Among them are the female singers Joni Mitchell, Carole King, Aretha Franklin, and Janis Joplin.

751 Larkin, Philip. All What Jazz; A Record Diary, 1961-68. New York: St. Martin's Press, 1970.
A collection of short articles which first appeared in the Daily Telegraph and which covered a wide variety of subjects on jazz including women such as Billie Holiday.

752 Larsen, Arved M. "The Contemporary Woman Composer." Pan Pipes 68:2, November 1975.
A symposium at Southern Connecticut State College. Four of America's women composers were in a panel discussion on the subject of women as composers. In addition, there was a film presentation plus a concert of some of their works.

753 Laufer, Beatrice. "A Woman Composer Speaks Out." ASCAP Today 1(2):9, 1967.
No woman composer has received the recognition that the well-known male composers of the twentieth century have. Although this discrimination in the form of apathy or polite tolerance is widespread, at least one group is recognizing women composers for their talents: the American Society of Composers, Authors and Publishers.

754 Laurie, J. "Alice Lloyd--Symbol of an Era." Variety 176:51, November 23, 1959.

755 Lawrence, Marjorie. Interrupted Melody; The Story

of My Life. Carbondale: Southern Illinois University Press, 1968.
The autobiography of the Australian singer who performed in many U.S. productions.

756 Lawrence, Robert. A Rage for Opera; Its Anatomy As Drawn from Life. New York: Dodd, Mead, 1971.
Chapter 3, "The Singers," looks at a number of American women who have become great performers.

757 _____. The World of Opera. New York: T. Nelson, 1956.
The American Marian Anderson and Maria Callas are among the principal operatic performers included in this work.

758 "Leave It to the Girls." Metronome 72:18-19, December 1956.

759 Lee, Janet A. "Essay on SA, or, Try a Chorus of Treble Voices." Music Ministry s2, 6:8-9, July 1974.
Ms. Lee shares some of her experiences as a conductor of a women's choir. A short repertoire is given at the end of the article.

760 Lees, Gene. "Passion of Malvina Reynolds." High Fidelity/Musical America 18:106, May 1968.
Mrs. Reynolds is the California folk singer who composed the popular song "Little Boxes," which spoke of suburban houses all made of "ticky-tacky."

761 Leff, L. J. "Madame Butterfly: The First Heroine." Opera News 40:24-26, April 3, 1976.
Blanche Bates is the opera singer discussed in this role.

762 "Lena Horne Scenes Out of 'Words' in Memphis." Variety 173:3, January 5, 1959.
The discrimination which Negro musicians have faced is described in this article.

763 Leonard, Neil. Jazz and the White Americans; The Acceptance of a New Art Form. Chicago: University of Chicago Press, 1962.
The music of Bessie Smith plus an examination of her lyrics are included in this work.

764 "Leontyne Price Closes Old Met and Reopens New." Variety 240:1, September 22, 1965.

765 "Leontyne's Latest." Time 77:83, April 7, 1960.

766 Lerman, Leo. "Girl on the Record." Mademoiselle 37:116, October 1953.

767 _____. "The Local Legend; Sweet Emma Barrett." Mademoiselle 68:150-151, February 1969.
    Emma Barrett, a seventy-year-old black singer, wore bells on her garters and shoes. She became a New Orleans legend and was still performing on Bourbon Street in 1969.

768 _____. "The New Divas." Mademoiselle 40:102-103, November 1954.
    Pictures and biographical sketches of twelve young women opera singers; all but two were Americans.

769 _____. "Soundest Sounds '74." Mademoiselle 79:170, May 1974.
    Twelve promising women musicians are discussed. Joni Mitchell is the most prominent member of the group.

770 "Let's Look at the Score." Instrumental Music 62:12, August 1963.
    Liza Redfield is discussed.

771 Levison, E. "Eartha Kitt Role in South Africa's Color Break-Thru." Variety 267:1, May 31, 1972.

772 Liesen, Philomene. "How Do You Look?" School Musician 45:54-55, June-July 1974.
    Hints for women band directors. A discussion of the attire that is appropriate for a woman who directs bands in concerts.

773 "Life Tours Europe with a College Choir." Life 33:46, August 11, 1952.
    A pictorial journal of the thirty-two-voice Smith College Girls Choir on a European concert tour.

774 "Lifestyle." American Home 73:8, October 1970.
    An interview with Dionne Warwick. This black singer relates her philosophy of life.

775 "Lipstick on the Bandwagon." Melody Maker 36:3, August 19, 1961.

776 Little, Lowell. "Should Girls Play Wind and Percussion Instruments?" Instrumentalist 12:49-51, September 1957.
   Little is the director of the Texas Woman's University Bands and speaks from experience in encouraging women to play wind and percussion instruments.

777 Livingstone, W. "Viva Diva!" Stereo Review 35:48, September 1975.
   Discussion of fans' loyalty to a favorite diva and how all their excitement, expressed by clapping and shouts, disturbs others at a performance.

778 Lomax, Alan. "The Passing of a Great Singer--Vera Hall." Sing Out 14:30, July 1964.
   Vera Hall, a black folk singer from Alabama, died in 1964. A short sketch of her life singing folk music is given, plus music and lyrics to one of her compositions.

779 _____. The Rainbow Sign. New York: Duell, Sloan and Pearce, 1959.
   Vera Hall was a Southern Negro folk singer whose life was chronicled in this work. Her name was changed to Nora in this book to protect her anonymity before her death in 1964.

780 London, George. "Prima Donnas I Have Sung Against." High Fidelity 7:43, March 1957.
   Mr. London reminisces about some of the great women opera singers with whom he has worked.

781 Longstreet, Stephen. Sportin' House; A History of the New Orleans Sinners and the Birth of Jazz. Los Angeles: Sherbourne Press, 1965.
   A unique examination of the relationship of jazz to the madames and their girls in the New Orleans sporting houses.

782 Lord, Bobby. Hit the Glory Road! Nashville: Broadman Press, 1969.
   Discusses American folk music singers.

783 Lowry, A. "Chamber Music for Women's Voices." Choral Journal 13:15, December 1972.

784 Luc-Gabrielle, Sister. "Nun's Story." Time 82:72, November 15, 1963.
  Sister Luc-Gabrielle and four other nuns from her convent recorded their songs on an album which sold well in Europe but not in the United States. However, by putting "Dominique" on a 45 rpm, it became a hit here and about $100,000 has been earned for the Dominicans to use for missionary work.

785 Lucas, B. "Minnie Riperton." Ebony 32:33, December 1976.

786 Lydon, Michael. "Janis Joplin Philosophy: Every Moment She Is What She Feels." New York Times Magazine February 23, 1969, p. 36.
  After becoming the top female rock singer with the group Big Brother and the Holding Company, Joplin decided to quit this group and form a new band with herself as leader. She also began singing heavier rhythm and blues instead of just rock.

787 _____. "Soul Kaleidoscope: Aretha at the Fillmore." Ramparts Magazine 10:30-39, October 1971.
  A review of Aretha Franklin's soul music performance at the Fillmore West in San Francisco. Her style is analyzed.

788 Lynn, Loretta. Loretta Lynn: Coal Miner's Daughter. Chicago: H. Regnery, 1976.
  The story of this country music singer's life.

789 Lyon, Hugh Lee. Leontyne Price; Highlights of a Prima Donna. New York: Vantage Press, 1973.
  A biography of this Negro opera singer's career with a list of principal events in her life plus discography. One section of the work is devoted to "Other Black Singers at the Metropolitan Opera House."

790 McCarrell, Lamar K. "The Impact of World War II upon the College Band." Journal of Band Research 10(1):3-8, 1973.
  One section of this article is addressed to "The Increased Use of Women in College Bands." During World War II, many all-male college bands were depleted, and the admission of girls became necessary for the survival of the organization.

791 McCracken, James, and Warfield, Sandra. A Star in the Family; An Autobiography in Diary Form. New York: Coward, McCann & Geoghegan, 1971.
McCracken and Warfield are operatic singers who are married to each other. This autobiography is their diary of 1969, providing insight into singers' lives in the world of opera.

792 McCutcheon, Lynn Ellis. Rhythm and Blues; An Experience and Adventure in Its Origin and Development. Arlington, Va.: Beatty, 1971.
The Supremes and Aretha Franklin are examples of women in rhythm and blues who have influenced this style of music.

793 _____. "Unsung Heroes Who Also Sang; Soul Singers." Negro History Bulletin 36:9-11, January 1973.

794 McDaniel, C. G. "Funeralizing Mahalia." Christian Century 89:253-254, March 1, 1972.

795 McDearmon, Kay. Mahalia, Gospel Singer. New York: Dodd, Mead, 1976.
This brief biography is juvenile literature. It tells of Jackson's career singing gospel songs.

796 McDonald, E. "Anna Moffo." House Beautiful 112:60-63, February 1970.
An interview with this American opera singer.

797 McDonough, Jack. "Ellen Bernstein, 2 Other Fems, Run San Francisco A&R Offices." Billboard 86:4, August 3, 1974.
The Columbia Records office in San Francisco is probably the only one in the nation being managed by women during 1974. Ms. Bernstein's first job as director was to earn the respect of artists and managers with whom Columbia had record contracts.

798 _____. "KSAN's Women: San Francisco Station Gains Listeners Via Their Efforts." Billboard 87:28, April 5, 1975.
Bonnie Simmonds is program director for KSAN, an FM station in San Francisco. Many other women hold responsible positions in this organization as well.

799 McElroy, George, and Stedman, Jane W. "Chorus

Lady." <u>Opera News</u> 38:10-13, February 16, 1974.

Margaret Hillis is conductor of the Chicago Symphony Chorus. Her preparation for this job is described and a typical rehearsal with the chorus is followed.

800 Mackin, Tom. "Women Song Writers." <u>Music Journal</u> 10:30, March 1952.

A survey of song literature written by women in all areas of music.

801 "Mahalia Jackson: 'Gospel Isn't Pop.'" <u>Down Beat</u> 30:12, August 15, 1963.

Jackson decries the use of gospel-like songs in night clubs for entertainment. As a devout person she admits to having made money singing gospel music, but asserts that she never brought the songs of God to a low level.

802 "Mahalia Jackson Says Rock & Jazz Have No Place in Church Rites." <u>Variety</u> 259:1, July 22, 1970.

803 "Mahalia Jackson's Constitution Hall." <u>Variety</u> 217:2, February 24, 1960.

804 Maier, Guy. "A Great Woman Composer? When?" <u>Etude</u> 72:21, May 1954.

Maier discusses the many reasons which may be responsible for the lack of female composers. He expects that there will be many in the future.

805 _____. "Shall I Major in Music? Long-View Suggestion for Girls at College." <u>Etude</u> 66:468, August 1948.

Dr. Maier usually encourages women to major in music because they can teach lessons in their community after they have married and raised their families.

806 Mainwaring, Fredrica. "Raise the Chorus." <u>Music Journal</u> 14:29, April 1956.

The problems and joys of organizing a women's chorus of homemakers and finally arriving at the point where a concert can be given is described.

807 "Male Maestro for Hub's First All-Femme Symph." <u>Variety</u> 236:1, September 9, 1964.

The Boston Women's Symphony Orchestra gave its first concert September 11, 1964. The conductor noted that women musicians comprised about 2 per cent of the 1,500 orchestra members in the U.S. and Canada, while 60 per cent of the student musicians in higher education are women.

808 Marcus, Greil. "How the Other Half Lives; The Best of Girl Group Rock." Let It Rock May 1974, pp. 24-25.

809 "Marian Anderson Free to Play Lyric, Balto; Board in Face-Saver." Variety 192:73, November 18, 1953.

810 Marsh, D. "Don't Touch That Dial: Women Beat the Airwaves Hollow." Creem Magazine 5:45, May 1974.
Discussion of women in the field of popular music.

811 "Martha and the Vandellas." Ebony 23:83, February 1968.
Martha Reeves and the Vandellas have moved out of the shadow of the similar all-girl trio, the Supremes. This article chronicles their rise to stardom.

812 Martin, Mary. My Heart Belongs. New York: William Morrow, 1976.
The actress and singer, Mary Martin, reminisces about her career in show business.

813 Marx, H. "We Note That (Mary Garden Asks Change in Education of Singers)." Music News 44:5, February 1952.

814 "Matter of Art, Not Sex." Time 106:59, November 10, 1975.
Among the women composers mentioned are the two Americans Antonia Brico (age 73) and Judith Somogi (age 34).

815 Matz, Mary Jane. "Decline of the Diva." Opera News 30:12-16, March 12, 1966.
Opera singers at one time were treated as celebrities. However, in recent years this adoration has been accorded to rock musicians.

816 "Maybelle Carter, Stoneman Interview in Hall of Fame."

Billboard 80:30, February 24, 1968.
Country music singers are discussed.

817 Mayor, Martin. "Marilyn Horne Becomes a Prima Donna." New York Times Magazine January 17, 1971, p. 14.
Although Miss Horne has sung secondary roles at the Metropolitan Opera, 1971 was the first time she performed in a primary role there.

818 _____. "Recordings; Sopranos." Esquire 75:30, February 1971.
A review of some of the world's foremost sopranos during 1971. Americans such as Beverly Sills are included.

819 Melanson, J. "Music, Not Lib, Is Main Deadly Nightshade Thrust." Billboard 87:23, July 5, 1975.
The rock group, The Deadly Nightshade, is composed of three women who want to emphasize their musical ability and not the fact that they are females. They have performed for women's rights rallies and they acknowledge their interest in this cause, but they want their talent to be the criterion for success.

820 Meltz, Ramona J. "Women in the Service Band." School Musician 42:74-75, December 1970.
This director of the Women's Army Corps Band at Fort McClellan, Alabama, outlines the qualifications and activities of an army band for women.

821 Merker, E. "The Case for Women in Brass." Musart 28(2):30-32, 1975.
This article on women who play brass instruments is reprinted from Leblanc World of Music, Fall 1975.

822 Merkling, Frank. "Do, Re to Diva." Mademoiselle 40:104, November 1954.
Opera singers relate the problems they encounter along the road to success. Included is an introduction to the study, scholarship and financial rewards of opera.

823 Merman, Ethel. Don't Call Me Madam. London: W. H. Allen, 1955.
The story of this American singer's life.

824 Meryman, R. "Tour of Two Great Throats." Life 68: 63, June 26, 1970.
　　Joan Sutherland and Marilyn Horne are the two singers who are analyzed.

825 "Met Triumph for Leontyne." Life 50:107-110, February 10, 1961.
　　Leontyne Price is the opera star at the Metropolitan who is noted for her success as a Negro singer.

826 Meyer, Hazel. Gold in Tin Pan Alley. Philadelphia: Lippincott, 1958.
　　Although this work concentrates on the monetary aspect of jazz, it refers to individuals such as Bessie Smith in the discussion.

827 Micklo, Ann Marie. "Women Is Losers; An Analysis of Females in Rock 'n' Roll." Senior Scholastic 98: 22, April 26, 1971.
　　Female artists have not had the opportunities to succeed in rock music that men have. There were some exceptions which fall into three categories: Joan Baez-type folk singers; the "Electric Ladies" like screamer Janis Joplin; and "Soul Singers" as Aretha Franklin. Micklo feels the Women's Liberation Movement is helping to achieve equal opportunities for women.

828 Milan, Judith. "On Stage: Joan Baez." Horizon 5:66-67, September 1962.
　　An examination of the style of Joan Baez's folk music of the 1950's and 1960's.

829 Miller, E. "Off the Record with the Supremes." Seventeen 25:280, August 1966.
　　An interview with this singing trio: Diana Ross, Mary Wilson, and Florence Ballard.

830 _____. "Singer Is the Song." Seventeen 32:72, November 1973.
　　Carole King talks about her music.

831 Miller, Philip L. "Over on the Distaff Side, Mostly; Miriam Gideon and Four Other Americans." American Record Guide 39:742-743, November 1972.
　　Record review of an album by the composers

Miriam Gideon, Louise Talma, Julia Smith, Mabel Daniels, and Burrill Phillips.

832 "Milwaukee Symphony Salute to Women in Music." Pan Pipes 68:3, November 1975.
    The Milwaukee Symphony gave a concert in 1975 in recognition of women in music. Details of the program are given.

833 Minnie Pearl; BB's Country Man of Year." Billboard 78:1, October 29, 1966.

834 Minson, M. B. "Her Eye Is on the Hit Parade." Profitable Hobbies 10:22, January 1954.
    Concerns women composers.

835 Mitchell, George. Blow My Blues Away. Baton Rouge: Louisiana State University Press, 1971.
    Three chapters are devoted to these women blues musicians: Rosa Lee Hill, Jessie Mae Brooks, and Ada Mae Anderson.

836 Moncrieff, Gladys. My Life of Song. Adelaide, Australia: Rigby, 1971.

837 Monson, Karen. "Contemp. Ch. Players." High Fidelity/Musical America 25:29, July 1975.
    Ms. Shulamit Ran's "Ensembles for 17" was performed at the University of Chicago's Contemporary Chamber Players' 1975 Fromm Concert. This Israeli woman is on the faculty at the University of Chicago.

838 Montagu, Ashley. "Why Wagner Was No Lady." High Fidelity 8:34, March 1958.
    An essay by an anthropologist on the biological and sociological reasons that may help explain the lack of great women composers.

839 Monteith, Ann K. "The Lebanon Valley College All-Girl Band." Instrumentalist 27:40, June 1973.
    This completely female band is possibly the only one in the U.S. in 1973. It was formed in 1934 to give girls an opportunity to participate in a band, since most bands at the time were entirely male.

840 Moore, Eleanor. "Unraveling Roberta." Saturday Review 55:56-60, June 17, 1972.

Roberta Flack's lifestyle is discussed in this article. She is a vivacious performer on stage singing rock music, but loves peace and quiet at home.

841 Moore, Gerald. "These Are the Mamas." Life 61:77-78, September 30, 1966.
An article on the rising stardom of Michelle Phillips and Cass Elliot, the two female members of the singing group, The Mamas and the Papas.

842 Moore, June. "Sex on the Podium." Instrumentalist 26:57-58, December 1971.
Discusses the attire of a woman conductor and its effect (good and bad) on the audience.

843 "More Than an Entertainer." Time 93:63, February 21, 1969.
Nina Simone, the Negro singer, is evaluated.

844 Morella, Joe, and Epstein, Edward Z. Judy; The Films and Career of Judy Garland. New York: Citadel Press, 1969.
A chronicle of Judy Garland's acting and singing career along with many photographs of her.

845 Morgan, Alfred Lindsay. "New Conductor for a Famous Orchestra." Etude 58:737, November 1940.
Izler Solomon conducted the sixty-five member Chicago Women's Symphony Orchestra in 1940. This was an active musical group which gave many concerts.

846 Morschauser, J. "Moppets: College Ladies of Rock." Look 30:56, June 14, 1966.
Four college women from Mount Holyoke who dressed like elegant ladies but didn't let it interfere with the wild rock music they played.

847 Morse, Charles. Carly Simon. Mankato, Minn.: Creative Education, 1975.
Carly Simon, a folk singer and composer, is discussed in this book for young people. The musical part of her life is emphasized.

848 _____. Roberta Flack. Mankato, Minn.: Creative Education, 1975.
A short biography for juveniles of the black singer Roberta Flack.

849 Morse, David. *Motown & the Arrival of Black Music.* London: Studio Vista, 1971.
   Motown is a company which concentrates on promoting black musicians. It became a very successful business in the 1960's by featuring such popular music groups as the Supremes and Martha and the Vandellas.

850 "Most Female Singers Present Songs That Should Be Done by Their Male Colleagues." *Music News* 43:4, March 1951.

851 "Most Promising Female Vocalist." *Billboard* 71:38, October 22, 1949 Suppl.

852 "Most Promising 'Newer' Female Vocalists." *Billboard* 62:27, October 7, 1950 Suppl.

853 Mothner, Ira. "Big Folk-Singers on Campus: Peter, Paul & Mary." *Look* 27:59-62, July 2, 1963.
   Short interviews with each member of the trio. Mary Travers started singing early by giving her first performance at age five.

854 "Moving on Up." *Newsweek* 79:49, February 7, 1972.
   Obituary of Mahalia Jackson using material drawn from her autobiography *Movin' on Up*. As the queen of gospel singers, she sang her way from a Louisiana shack to the White House.

855 "Moving on Up." *Time* 99:89, February 7, 1972.
   A synopsis of Mahalia Jackson's life as a gospel singer. She sang these songs because she felt they expressed hope and did not sing blues because she felt they were too full of despair.

856 Mueller, John Henry. *The American Symphony Orchestra; A Social History of Musical Taste.* Bloomington: Indiana University Press, 1951.
   The subjects of all-women orchestras and the issue of admitting women to previously all-male orchestras are treated on pp. 308-310. A count of women on the rosters of professional orchestras of the major American cities during World War II showed a respectable number; this was probably due to the reduced numbers of male musicians.

857 Murphy, R. "On Stage: Leontyne Price." *Horizon* 3:72-73, March 1961.

858 "Music People." Seventeen 34:38, January 1975.
Stephanie Mills, a black singer is discussed.

859 "Music Women Form New NAWM Group." Billboard 87:48, September 27, 1975.

860 "Musicians' Wives Organize in L.A." Down Beat 27:12-13, November 24, 1960.
Wives of musicians in Southern California have formed a social and philanthropic organization. Proceeds of their activities will go "toward the goal of establishing a relief fund for the families of needy musicians, a trust fund for music scholarships, and, eventually, a relief home."

861 "Music's Wonder Woman." Time 106:52-65, November 10, 1975.
This cover story examines Sarah Caldwell, the conductor, and her recent success with the Opera Company of Boston.

862 Musser, Willard I. "Female Oboists." Woodwind World 10:5, April 1971.
This article discusses the accusation that women oboists in major orchestras make more mistakes than men. One man states that he thinks this is due to women's being more emotional than men. Other reasons for rejecting women oboists include their being distracted by other women's attire in the audience, trying to attract a male orchestral member, or the possibility of catching her high heels on the music stand.

863 Myrus, Donald. I Like Jazz. New York: Macmillan Co., 1964.
Women blues singers such as Bessie Smith, Ma Rainey, Ethel Waters, and Mahalia Jackson are discussed in this story of jazz.

864 "NFMC Women Composers." Showcase 42(4):61-62, 1963.

865 "Nancy Holloway." Ebony 20:33, January 1965.
This black singer from Cleveland has been successful in European night clubs, especially France. For that reason she has been more interested in continuing her performances there than in the U.S.

866 Nanry, Charles. <u>American Music: From Storyville to Woodstock</u>. New Brunswick, N.J.: Transaction Books, 1972.
   Essays on popular music in America of sociological significance. Jazz is emphasized along with singers such as Janis Joplin.

867 Napier, Simon A. "The Unknowns (No. 7): Hattie Hart--Allen Shaw." <u>Blues Unlimited</u> 32:7-8, April 1966.
   These two blues singers from Memphis teamed up in 1934 to record in New York.

868 Neff, Robert, and Connor, Anthony. <u>Blues</u>. Boston: David R. Godine, 1975.
   Interviews with blues musicians who performed during the past forty years (1930's-1970's). Rather than a history of the blues, these musicians talk of their experiences in the field. Black women such as Ester Phillips are included.

869 Nelson, J. "A Melody for International Women's Year." <u>Instrumental Musician</u> 74:8, July 1975.

870 Nelson, Mary Jarman. "Why Not a Mothers' Study Group? Experiment with Mothers of Pre-School Children." <u>Etude</u> 58:22, January 1940.
   Ms. Nelson tells of her experience in teaching musical concepts to mothers of young children so they could help their children's education.

871 Nettl, Paul. "Women in Music." <u>Music Journal</u> 18:8, February 1960.
   Women in music have a better chance to achieve in America than in any of the European countries according to Nettl. Even so, this sketch of women musicians of the past shows that there were always some women musicians being recognized on both continents.

872 "New Chamber Music Society Founded." <u>Music of the West</u> 16:14, September 1960.
   The Women's Chamber Music Society of Los Angeles was founded in 1960 by Mrs. Vahdah Olcott Bickford who was an authority on classic guitar. Included are reviews by Mrs. Bickford of the organization's first three concerts.

873 "New Plans Announced for Women's Symphony." Musical America 69:16, July 1949.

874 "The New Prima Donna--at Work." High Fidelity/Musical America 15:41, February 1965.
 An article decrying the unpopular temperaments of opera stars (chiefly women) of the past. Today's first ladies of the opera are working very hard in a professional manner to produce top quality results.

875 Newman, Mrs. M. W. "Women's Association Educational Projects--New Trends." American Symphony Orchestra League Newsletter 20(3-4):21-22, 1969.
 "Ten panelists reported on educational projects in which their women's associations had participated."

876 Newman, Shirlee Petkin. Marian Anderson: Lady from Philadelphia. Philadelphia: Westminster Press, 1966.
 The story of this black woman's rise to fame as an opera singer.

877 _____. Mary Martin on Stage. Philadelphia: Westminster Press, 1969.
 The biography of Mary Martin which tells of her career as a singer and entertainer in the theater.

878 Nikolaieff, George. "Stephanie Mills." Senior Scholastic 105:36-37, September 26, 1974.
 An interview with Stephanie Mills, a 15-year old singer from Brooklyn who sounds somewhat like Diana Ross.

879 Noble, Helen Klaffky. Life with the Met. New York: G. P. Putnam's Sons, 1954.
 Autobiographical view of the New York Metropolitan Opera by Noble.

880 Norcott, B. J. "Girl Orchestra." Life with Music 3:14-15, January 1950.

881 Northcutt, John Orlando. Magic Valley, the Story of Hollywood Bowl. Los Angeles: Fashion Press, 1967.
 Chapter 23 is "Women's Important Role; Distaff Side of the Bowl." It is noted that many women have performed in the Hollywood Bowl over the years.

882 "Notes from a Bearded Lady: The American Woman Composer." Instrumental Musician 74:9, July 1975.

883 Novak, B. J. "Opening Doors in Music." Negro History Bulletin 34:10-14, January 1971.
　　Negro singers are noted for their successes in being accepted for opera roles.

884 "Now One Is Speechless." Time 64:87, October 18, 1954.
　　Marian Anderson, a Negro contralto, has been the first Negro to be signed at the Metropolitan Opera.

885 "Oklahoma City Has a Lot of Talented Musical Women Who Give the City a Special Flavor." Billboard 85: 012, November 19, 1973.
　　Country, gospel, and popular music has its share of women performers as well as women in the managing and recording areas of music in Oklahoma City.

886 Oliver, Marie. Let's Have Music; The Place and Planning of Music in Program. 2nd ed. New York: Woman's Press, 1948.
　　Chiefly consists of articles from the magazine, The Woman's Press, telling of Y.W.C.A. music activities.

887 "One-Woman Shows Sizzling on B'Way; Liza, Bette Whammo." Variety 273:2, December 12, 1973.
　　Liza Minelli and Bette Midler are singing their way to success.

888 "Opera's Gain." Newsweek 44:96, October 18, 1954.
　　Marian Anderson, an American contralto, was the first Negro singer to perform at the Metropolitan Opera House in New York.

889 Oppenheimer, Peer J. "The Unstoppable Mama Cass." Family Weekly August 2, 1970, p. 14.

890 Orloff, Katherine. Rock 'n' Roll Woman. Los Angeles: Nash Pub., 1974.
　　Interviews with Nicoel Barclay, Toni Brown, Rita Coolidge, Grace Slick, and others in rock music.

891 Orth, Maureen. "Pointers on Parade." Newsweek 82: 78, August 29, 1973.

An examination of the sudden success of the four Pointer Sisters--Ruth, Anita, Bonnie, and June.

892 Osborne, Conrad L. "The Callas Master Classes." High Fidelity/Musical America 22:MA12-13, June 1972.
Maria Callas, the great American soprano, has been teaching master classes at the Juilliard School of Music in New York. Students auditioned to be in her class. Osborne's conclusion was that "the vast majority of the singers were simply not equipped for the work."

893 Oster, Harry. Living Country Blues. Detroit: Folklore Associates, 1969.
An extensive history of country blues which includes women composers and performers such as Billie Pierce and Sally Dotson.

894 Ostransky, Leroy. The Anatomy of Jazz. Seattle: University of Washington Press, 1960.
An analysis of the stylistic characteristics that make up jazz along with short references to musicians' styles such as that of Bessie Smith.

895 "Our Starlets in Opera." Newsweek 53:116-118, April 6, 1959.
The U.S. has about ten major opera companies besides the Metropolitan. Therefore, opportunities are limited for newcomers to perform. The American hopefuls such as Betty Hodges, Margherita Roberti, and Anna Moffo are singing in European opera productions to gain valuable experience.

896 Paige, Raymond. "Why Not Women in Orchestras?" Etude 70:14-15, January 1952.
Paige relates that women are members of many orchestras during 1952 and the discrimination that they have faced in the past is rapidly diminishing.

897 "Paige Guertin Becomes First Woman Salesman in Band Instrument Industry." School Musician 44:40, October 1972.
This flutist and teacher is the first woman to be appointed to represent a musical instrument company. She is educational director and distributor in Southern California for K. G. Gemeinhardt Company, Inc.

898 Panassié, Hughes. *The Real Jazz*. Rev. ed. New York: Barnes, 1960.
   In the preface Panassié states that he has changed his opinion about some musicians since his earlier book, *Hot Jazz*. Women jazz singers are discussed on pp. 193-197.

899 "Paris Bound with Diahann." *Life* 51:67-68, November 3, 1961.
   Diahann Carroll, who rose to stardom with her singing is now acting in the film *Paris Blues* which incorporates Duke Ellington's jazz.

900 Parker, D. C. "A Group of Violinists." *Strad* 69:362, February 1959.
   Discusses women as musicians.

901 Partridge, Robert. "Dialogue: MM Special on Women in Rock." *Melody Maker* 48:36-38, November 10, 1973.

902 "Passionate and Sloppy." *Time* 98:71, August 9, 1968.
   The rock and blues singer Janis Joplin is reviewed.

903 Paul, Doris A. "This I Believe." *Music Journal* 12:83, March 1954.
   Ms. Paul contends that women are not joining choruses to get away from the drudgery of housework but to experience the aesthetic pleasure of singing good music. As a director she chooses songs that are of good quality to fulfill this need as well as to be pleasing entertainment during their concerts.

904 "People Are Talking About ... por *Vogue*." *Vogue* 140:108-109, November 1, 1962.
   Leontyne Price, the American Negro opera star, is one of the people of note according to this article.

905 Perle, George. "The Music of Mariam Gideon." *American Composers Alliance Bulletin* 7(4):2-9, 1958.
   A study of Gideon's compositions with musical examples to aid in the analyzation. Includes a list of her works and comments by the press.

906 Peters, A. "Ordeal of Tammi Terrell." *Ebony* 25:94, November 1969.

907 Peters, Roberta. *A Debut at the Met.* New York: Meredith Press, 1967.
   The story of this soprano's struggle to achieve her goal of attaining a position at the Metropolitan Opera. She succeeded in becoming a principal singer there.

908 Pfautsch, Lloyd. "Sing Us No Sad Songs." *Pan Pipes* 57(2):17-19, 1965.
   Dr. Pfautsch decries the lack of good music written specifically for women's choirs. He encourages American composers to write for this medium and gives a short list of works by Americans that are now available.

909 Philips, Mary. "Notes on the IWY Tribune International Women's Year." *Triangle* 70(1):27-28, 1975.
   There was little discussion on women's status in music or in any of the fine arts during the International Women's Year Conference held in Mexico City. However, this article does report on the information that was available.

910 Phillips, Karen. "Women Musicians Offer Advice." *Music Journal* 32:18-19, March 1974.
   Many current serious musicians offer advice to others of their sex who want to achieve in this field.

911 Podis, Eunice. "Musical Careers for Women." *Music Journal* 18:22, October 1960.
   At this time the prospects are brightest for vocalists since the Metropolitan Opera includes many American women singers. A career as an instrumentalist is more difficult to attain. Mrs. Podis shares some of her experiences as a concert pianist.

912 Pollock, Bruce. *In Their Own Words.* New York: Macmillan, 1975.
   Four women rock and popular musicians are interviewed: Felice Bryant, Buffy Sainte-Marie, Melanie Safka, and Linda Creed.

913 Ponzo, Marie. "Women's Lib and the Lyric Muse." *Opera News* 36:13, January 8, 1972.
   Operatic heroines' characters are analyzed in relation to the Women's Liberation Movement.

914 Poppy, John. "Janis Joplin: Big Brother's White Soul."

Look 32:60-62, September 3, 1968.
> Janis Joplin is the lead female singer of the rock band Big Brother and the Holding Company.

915 Porter, Andrew. "Musical Events; Ladies' Night." New Yorker 51:151-154, November 24, 1975.
> Sarah Caldwell recently conducted the New York Philharmonic in works written exclusively by women.

916 "Pride and Joy of Orange, Tex. Is the Wonderful Girls' School Band." Life 9:48-50, October 14, 1940.
> This band consisted of 144 female members.

917 "Prima Donna from Mississippi." Ebony 16:96, April 1961.
> Leontyne Price's debut at the Metropolitan Opera in Il Trovatore is reviewed.

918 "Queen Bees." Newsweek 71:77-78, January 15, 1968.
> Female singers in rock groups are becoming forces. Prominent ones include Cass Elliot, Janis Joplin, and Grace Slick.

919 Ragan, Elnor S. "Lady Luthiers? Yes!" American String Teacher 23(4):46, 1973.
> Women's Liberation has opened new careers for many. Ragan teaches and repairs stringed instruments. She encourages other women string players to make their own repairs.

920 Reed, R. "Leslie Uggams Polishes Up Her New Image." Good Housekeeping 166:50, April 1968.

921 "Report Card." Time 100:52, December 4, 1972.
> Cornell University has decided to allow women to audition for its Glee Club although women have been on campus since 1872. However, only tenor or bass voices can be accepted since the club intends to continue using music written for male voices.

922 Revelli, William D. "Women Can Teach Instrumental Music!" Etude 61:311, May 1943.
> More women are teaching instrumental music, which was previously an all-male field. The shortage of men for teaching positions because of the war made this transition to women teachers a smooth one.

923 Ricapito, Joseph A. "Mothers' Club." School Musician 31:38, February 1960.
 This music supervisor expresses his thoughts on the value of mothers' clubs in promoting music education in the public schools.

924 Richter, M. M. "A Salute to American Women Composers--1970 NFMC 'Parade' Concert in New York." Music Clubs Magazine 49(4):13-15, 1970.

925 Riddle, Almeda. A Singer and Her Songs; Almeda Riddle's Book of Ballads. Baton Rouge: Louisiana State University Press, 1970.
 The autobiography of this Arkansas lady who has sung and collected ballads all her life. Some music and lyrics are included in the discussion of American ballads.

926 Ritchie, Jean. The Singing Family of the Cumberlands. New York: Oxford University Press, 1955.
 Jean Ritchie relates the story of her family in Kentucky and of the folk music they were noted for singing.

927 Rittenhouse, Carl H. "Masculinity and Feminity in Relation to Preferences in Music." Ph.D. dissertation, Stanford University, 1952.

928 Rizzo, Francis. "Callas Class: Juilliard School." Opera News 36:14-16, April 15, 1972.
 An account of Maria Callas's master classes conducted at the Juilliard School of Music in 1971. She worked with some of the most promising vocal students.

929 Roach, Hildred. Black American Music: Past and Present. Boston: Crescendo Publishing Co., 1973.
 Biographical information about many black women who have influenced American music. Composers such as Margaret Bond and Undine Moore are discussed as well as famous opera singers such as Leontyne Price and Marian Anderson.

930 Roberts, Joan. Never Alone. New York: McMullen Books, 1954.
 An autobiography.

931 Roberts, John S. Black Music of Two Worlds. New

York: W. Morrow, 1974.
   This book traces the history of Afro-American music. The subject is so broad that few details about women are given except for the most important individuals, such as Bessie Smith.

932 Robinson, Francis. "Pedigree of the Prima Donna." Theatre Arts 41:82, January 1957.
   The temperaments of several women singers are explored. However, these same temperamental divas were usually well behaved at the Metropolitan Opera House. Some of the most memorable antics are disclosed.

933 Robinson, Louie. "Divine Sarah." Ebony 30:94, April 1975.
   A study of Sarah Vaughan's long career singing in jazz.

934 _____. "First Lady of Jazz." Ebony 17:131, November 1961.
   Ella Fitzgerald gives one of her few interviews. She relates how she first became involved in singing with jazz bands.

935 _____. "Nancy Wilson." Ebony 21:140, May 1966.
   This black singer is also a busy businesswoman and mother. Her hit album "Like in Love" was a springboard to other jobs as TV guest appearances and Las Vegas shows.

936 _____. "Why Diana Ross Left the Supremes." Ebony 25:120-126, February 1970.

937 "Rock 'n' Roll's Leading Lady." Time 104:59-62, December 16, 1974.
   Joni Mitchell's childhood and her break into the entertainment field are told.

938 "Rockers' Groupies Spark Film Trend." Variety 257:53, December 17, 1969.

939 Rodnitzky, Jerome L. "Songs of Sisterhood: The Music of Women's Liberation." Popular Music & Society 4(2):77, 1975.
   The feminist singers are stressing lyrics that raise the consciousness of women, such as Helen

Rosie and Liberation

Reddy's hit "I Am Woman." This article emphasizes feminist recordings and some of the women who have made them.

940 Roesch, C. B. "The Plight of the Woman Symphonic Player." Music Clubs Magazine 31:5, March 1952.

941 Rogers, C. "Mahalia Jackson: Saturday Night Rhythms and Sunday Morning Lyrics." Christian Century 89: 241-242, March 1, 1972.

942 Romaguoll, M. "Try and Stop Me." Choir Guide 4:39, June 1951.
Woman organists are discussed.

943 "Ronettes." Ebony 22:184, November 1966.
"Rock 'n' roll girls' trio teams up with the Beatles on a whirlwind, 14-city, U.S. entertainment tour."

944 Rorem, Ned. Critical Affairs; A Composer's Journal. New York: G. Braziller, 1970.
Chapter 9, "Ladies Music," expresses Rorem's perception of the woman as composer and the reasons behind her rise in popularity and public acceptance in the 1950's.

945 _____. Music and People. New York: Braziller, 1968.
Short essays in the format of a diary. Rorem's "Twelfth Interlude: Recalling Martha" consists of reminiscences of Martha Graham the dancer. His first job was as an accompanist for Graham's classes.

946 _____. The New York Diary. New York: Braziller, 1967.
Rorem's diary includes memories of some women with whom he worked, such as the sopranos Virginia Fleming and Ellen Faull.

947 _____. Pure Contraption: A Composer's Essays. New York: Holt, Rinehart and Winston, 1974.
Rorem's thoughts on musicians he has known such as Maria Callas and Billie Holiday.

948 _____. "Women: Artist or Artist-ess?" Vogue 155:172, April 1, 1970.
"Why can women write, paint, dance, perform -- but not compose music?" Rorem examines some possible reasons for the lack of women composers.

949 Rosen, Judith, and Rubin-Rabson, Grace. "Why Haven't Women Become Great Composers." High Fidelity/Musical America 23:46-52, February 1973.
   A feminist and a psychologist examine the lack of women composers in the past. Ms. Rosen feels men have squelched women in the field. Ms. Rubin-Rabson feels women lack the ultimate creative spark necessary for great compositions.

950 Rosen, Marjorie. "Antonia Brico: The Orchestra Is Her Instrument." Ms. 3:81, December 1974.
   A film has been made of this conductor's life: "Antonia: A Portrait of the Woman." In this interview, Brico tells of her long career as a conductor and how she founded the New York Women's Symphony in 1934. She is still actively conducting in 1974.

951 Rosenthal, Harold D. Great Singers of Today. London: Calder & Boyars, 1966.

952 _____. Sopranos of Today: Studies of Twenty-Five Opera Singers. London: J. Calder, 1956.

953 Rotante, A. "Discography of Lynn Hope." Record Research 79:9, October 1966.
   Lynn Hope is active in the field of jazz.

954 Roth, Henry. "Women and the Violin." Strad 83:551, March 1973.
   A discussion of the history of violin playing by women and the feelings against it. However, women did excel in this area and many are listed, including the American Eudice Shapiro.

955 Roussel, Hubert. The Houston Symphony Orchestra: 1913-1971. Austin: University of Texas Press, 1972.
   Women were instrumental in the formation of the Houston Symphony as officers and directors. The Women's Committee has been a vital part of this organization through the years.

956 Rubenstein, Raeanne. Honkytonk Heroes; A Photo Album of Country Music. New York: Harper & Row, 1975.
   Many country and western singers are included in this book which largely consists of photographs. The families of some of the singers are pictured.

957 Rushmore, Robert. The Singing Voice. New York: Dodd, Mead & Co., 1971.
Many women singers of the 1970's are referred to in the chapters on operatic voices.

958 Russell, Tony. Blacks, Whites, and Blues. New York: Stein and Day, 1970.
There are a few references to women blues musicians such as Clara Smith and Sara Martin who played the banjo.

959 Ryder, G. A. "Black Women in Song: Some Socio-Cultural Images; Address Oct. 1975." Negro History Bulletin 39:601-603, May 1976.

960 Saal, Hubert. "Girls, Letting Go; Rock Song Writers." Newsweek 74:68-71, July 14, 1969.

961 _____. "Sound of Women; New York Philharmonic Concert." Newsweek 86:83, November 24, 1975.
The New York Philharmonic combined with the magazine, Ms., to present a concert of music written only by women. Sarah Caldwell conducted with program which included works by women such as Ruth Crawford Seeger and Louise Talma.

962 _____. "Spirit of Mary Lou." Newsweek 78:67, December 20, 1971.
Mary Lou Williams, a foremost jazz musician, has been composing a mass.

963 _____ and Kuflik, A. "Music, Maestra." Newsweek 86:52-53, August 18, 1975.

964 Sabin, Robert. "Adele Marcus: The Challenge of Teaching." Musical America 83:53, February 1963.
Miss Marcus has been a piano teacher to students such as Byron Janis. She divulged her philosophy of teaching.

965 _____. "Leontyne Price Triumphs in Debut in Trovatore." Musical America 81:30-31, February 1961.
The black operatic singer received excellent reviews for her performance at the Metropolitan Opera. It was not too long ago that Marian Anderson broke the racial barrier and became the first one of her race to sing a major role at the Metropolitan.

966 "Saks and Saxon." Music & Artists 4(1):42, 1971.
   Ms. Toby Saks and Ms. Michele Saxon are two talented string musicians who have joined the New York Philharmonic. Saks plays the cello and Saxon plays the double bass.

967 "A Salute to America's Lady Professional Instrumentalists." School Musician 39:3, January 1968.
   Women instrumentalists in America are no longer excluded from the symphonic bands and orchestras. The magazine salutes outstanding women instrumentalists of the 1967 Detroit Concert Band as well as all other ladies in this field.

968 "A Salute to Women Composers." Pan Pipes 67:4-7, January 1975.
   A special display in the library of Northwestern University was devoted to women composers such as Louise Talma, Miriam Gideon, and Ruth Crawford Seeger.

969 Saminsky, Lazare. Living Music of the Americas. New York: Howell, Soskin and Crown, 1949.
   Two women composers of serious music are worth noting in the opinion of Saminsky: Vivian Fine and Miriam Gideon.

970 Sander, Ellen. "Rock and Roll Woman." Crawdaddy 8:25-30, April 2, 1972.

971 _____. Trips; Rock Life in the Sixties. New York: Scribner's, 1973.
   Women rock musicians are included in this work chiefly in regard to specific albums they have recorded.

972 Sanders, Charles L. "Aretha; A Close-Up Look at Sister Superstar." Ebony 29:124, December 1971.
   Aretha Franklin, a singer, pianist, and songwriter, is interviewed.

973 Sargeant, Winthrop. Divas. New York: Coward, McCann & Geoghegan, 1973.
   The book is divided into six chapters, one being devoted to each of the following Metropolitan Opera stars: Joan Sutherland, Marilyn Horne, Beverly Sills, Birgit Nilsson, Leontyne Price, and Eileen Farrell.

974 _____. "Musical Events; A Great Night." New Yorker 36:100, February 4, 1961.
A review of Leontyne Price's role as Leonora at her Metropolitan Opera debut.

975 _____. "Soprano's Progress." Life 18:47, March 26, 1945.
Jean Carlton from Des Moines began her operatic career with a debut in New York. All the training that is necessary just to reach this goal is noted, and the New York concert often determines the start or finish of a career.

976 Sarlin, Bob. Turn It Up! (I Can't Hear the Words): The Best of the New Singer/Songwriters. New York: Simon and Schuster, 1973.
Joni Mitchell and Laura Nyro are among the "Songpoets" examined in this work based chiefly on interviews.

977 Schiffman, Jack. Uptown; The Story of Harlem's Apollo Theatre. New York: Cowles Book Co., 1971.
Many black women were regular performers at the Apollo Theatre, such as Billie Holiday and the gospel singer Sister Rosetta Tharpe.

978 Schonberg, Harold C. "Ho-Yo-To-Ho! A New Bruennhilde." New York Times Magazine January 10, 1960, p. 17.
Opera singers were expected to be of generous proportions, the reasoning being that a large body usually results in a big sound. Wagnerian operas need full-sounding voices and ladies of ample girth have usually filled those roles. However, the much trimmer Wagnerian stars of the 1950's are proving that they can produce the sound needed.

979 Seagle, Helen. "Stevens Opening Soloist with San Antonio Symphony." Musical America 77:40, December 1, 1957.
Risë Stevens, a Metropolitan Opera mezzo-soprano, gave a concert during 1957 with the San Antonio Symphony which is under the direction of Jeannette Levi who was the first woman concertmaster of a major U.S. symphony.

980 Seeger, Peter. The Incompleat Folksinger. New York:

Simon and Schuster, 1972.
   An extensive history of folk music during the twentieth century with information on a number of women composers.

981 Seligman, Paul. Debuts & Farewells; A Two-Decade Photographic Chronicle of the Metropolitan Opera. New York: Knopf, 1972.
   A book of photographs including many prominent women singers.

982 Selner, J. C. "Women in the Church Choir." Catholic Choirmaster 35:109, September 1949.

983 Seltzer, George. The Professional Symphony Orchestra in the United States. Metuchen, N.J.: Scarecrow Press, 1975.
   Women's associations and the part they play in supporting American orchestras are treated in this work.

984 "Serious Matter." Newsweek 59:81, February 26, 1962.
   One of the best-known music teachers in the world conducted the New York Philharmonic in observance of her seventy-fifth birthday in 1962. Nadia Boulanger also conducted the Boston Symphony in 1938.

985 "Seven Glamor Girls and a Clown Wind Up Successful Opera Season." Life 10:38-39, March 31, 1941.
   Grace Moore, Gladys Swartout, and Risë Stevens were attractive American singers who finished the Metropolitan's 1941 season with Salvatore Baccaloni, a comic bass.

986 "Sex and the Promotion Girl." Billboard 83:8, January 2, 1971.
   There were five women record promoters in Los Angeles during 1971. An interview with two of them showed that women could be successful in this field which was recently all male.

987 Shapiro, Lynne D. "Into Pop Music, 'Fanny' First." Ms. 2:78-80, February 1974.
   Traces the origin of the rock music group, Fanny, composed of four young women.

988 Shapiro, Nat, and Hentoff, Nat. Hear Me Talkin' to Ya; The Story of Jazz As Told by the Men Who Made It. New York: Dover, 1966, c1955.
Quotations from jazz musicians about themselves and about famous musicians with whom they were acquainted. Chapter 14 is entirely about one woman: "Bessie Smith--the Empress of the Blues."

989 _____ and _____. Jazz Makers. New York: Rinehart, 1957.
This is a collection of short biographies of twenty-one jazz musicians. Two women are included: Bessie Smith and Billie Holiday.

990 Shapiro, S. "Rock Around the Crotch." Crawdaddy 48:68-69, May 1975.
Concerns women musicians in rock music.

991 Shaw, Arnold. The Rock Revolution. New York: Crowell-Collier Press, 1969.
Aretha Franklin, Dionne Warwick and Janis Joplin are women musicians who had an impact on rock and roll music.

992 _____. The Rockin' 50s; The Decade That Transformed the Pop Music Scene. New York: Hawthorn Books, 1974.
A thorough examination of the popular music of the 1950's. Patti Page, Brenda Lee, and Sarah Vaughan are among the long list of singers discussed.

993 _____. Trouble with Cinderella. New York: Farrar, Straus, 1950.

994 _____. The World of Soul; Black America's Contribution to the Pop Music Scene. New York: Cowles Book Co., 1970.
Many black women have contributed to the history of American popular music.

995 Shawe-Taylor, D. "Musical Events." New Yorker 49:52, December 31, 1973.
A selection of the ten greatest opera singers of this century are discussed. Singers such as Maria Callas will possibly be commemorated on postage stamps.

996 "She Who Is Ella." Time 84:86, November 27, 1964.
Ella Fitzgerald's career is reviewed.

997 Sheean, Vincent. "Spiritual Ground." <u>Opera News</u> 28:22-23, March 28, 1964.
   A critique of the qualities of Leontyne Price's voice.

998 Shelton, Robert. <u>The Country Music Story; A Picture History of Country and Western Music.</u> Indianapolis: Bobbs-Merrill Co., 1966.
   There are many women singers in country and western music.

999 Shepherd, Jack. "Beauty on the Trumpet." <u>Look</u> 29: M8-11, March 23, 1965.
   Carole Dawn Reinhart is the only female in the Juilliard Orchestra's brass section.

1000 Sherman, John K. "Woman Harpist or Cellist Is Top Sight at Concerts." <u>American String Teacher</u> 12(2): 1-2, 1962.
   Mr. Sherman comments on the beauty of a woman playing a harp or cello at a concert, as opposed to the less pleasing sight of a woman blasting on a brass instrument or pounding on a drum.

1001 Sherman, R. "Cleveland Women's Symphony Orchestra." <u>Instrumental Music</u> 67:5, December 1968.

1002 Shirley, George. "Black Performer; From the Minstrels to the Met." <u>Opera News</u> 35:6-13, January 30, 1971.
   Marian Anderson first performed in the New York Metropolitan Opera in 1955. Since that time opportunities have increased for other black performers in opera.

1003 Short, Bobby. "I Remember Ivie; Excerpt from Black and White Baby." <u>Saturday Review</u> 54:50, February 27, 1971.
   A review of Ivie Mary Anderson's talent as a jazz singer.

1004 "Shortage of Gal Band Singers." <u>Variety</u> 179:41, August 9, 1950.

1005 "Showbiz Sexes War in Offing? Fems Show Discrimination False." <u>Billboard</u> 61:22, November 5, 1949.
   Jo Staffard's manager has proof that women have

not been given the same opportunities as men in music. The radio field has discriminated against women performers the most, so women musicians have had to make personal appearance tours to prove their popularity.

1006 Shumsky, Ellen. "Womansong: Bringing It All Back Home." Sing Out 22:9-11, January-February 1974.
This feminist writer and singer feels that there has been much discrimination against women both as singers and as subject matter of songs. She is attempting to lift this oppression of women through her songs and articles.

1007 "Sibyl with Guitar." Time 80:54, November 23, 1962.
Folk singers jam together in their hootenannies as folk music becomes increasingly popular across the nation. Joan Baez is one of the leaders of this movement and her influence is extensive.

1008 "Sigma Alpha Iota Composers." Pan Pipes 63(2):39, 1971.

1009 "Sigma Alpha Iotas Are Founders." Pan Pipes 61:22-23, May 1969.
A list of SAI leaders in the music field from 1903-1969.

1010 Silberman, M. "Sarah Caldwell's New National Opera in Strong Road Start at Indianapolis." Variety 248:64, September 20, 1967.

1011 Sills, Beverly. "Singer Beverly Sills Talks about Opera and America." U.S. News & World Report 81:65, October 25, 1976.

1012 Silverman, Jerry. The Liberated Woman's Songbook. New York: Macmillan Co., 1971.

1013 Simon, Carly. Carly Simon Complete: Songs, Pictures, Words. New York: Alfred A. Knopf, 1975.
Interviews with Carly Simon over a period of several years, plus a pictorial history of her life. Most of the book is comprised of the songs she has written.

1014 Simon, G. "Mahalia Jackson; Veteran Gospel Singer

Thinks Jazz Should Have a Soul." Metronome 70: 16, December 1954.

1015 Simon, George Thomas. The Big Bands. New York: Macmillan Co., 1967.
In the big band era women were almost exclusively featured as singers. One chapter, "The Vocalists," discusses the ladies who sang with well-known dance orchestras, such as Doris Day with Les Brown's band. One exception to these all-male bands was Phil Spitalny's Hour of Charm Orchestra which was composed of about twenty-six female musicians (who reportedly neither played well nor looked good).

1016 _____. Simon Says; The Sights and Sounds of the Swing Era, 1935-1955. New Rochelle, N.Y.: Arlington House, 1971.
Women such as Dinah Shore were especially prominent as singers with dance bands during the swing era.

1017 Simpson, Harold. Singers to Remember. Lingfield, England: Oakwood Press, 1972.
Helen Traubel is one of the few Americans treated in this collection of short biographies plus discography of prominent opera singers.

1018 "Skylark & Golden Calves." Time 77:45, February 3, 1961.
Leontyne Price's roles in opera are discussed.

1019 Slater, Jack. "They Update the Past." Ebony 29:103, December 1973.
The Pointer Sisters of Oakland, California, were four backup singers until they became popular with their forties style at a Los Angeles engagement.

1020 "Slurs to Mahalia & India Dance Troupe Cue Fresh Racial Picketing in N.C." Variety 225:1, December 13, 1961.
Discrimination suffered by Mahalia Jackson is explored.

1021 "Small WAVE Washes Away Naval Tradition." Ebony 27:124, October 1972.
"Evangeline Baily becomes first female member of Navy band."

1022 Smith, Catherine Parons. "A Bicentennial Look at Women in American Music." Triangle 69(4):2-4, 1975.
A two hundred year survey of American women's contributions in the field of music.

1023 Smith, E. R. "The Film Career of Mamie Smith." Record Research 65:3, December 1964.
Jazz is incorporated in moving pictures.

1024 Smith, Kate. Upon My Lips a Song. New York: Funk & Wagnalls, 1960.
Kate Smith, the singer, shares her memories and experiences in this autobiography.

1025 "So She Up and Wrote a Song." American Magazine 154:51, December 1952.

1026 Somma, Robert. No One Waved Good-bye; A Casualty Report on Rock and Roll. New York: Outerbridge & Dienstfrey, 1971.
Discusses rock musicians who have died after they became successful, such as Janis Joplin.

1027 "Songs to Live By." Time 98:84, December 6, 1971.
The lyrics of Dory Previn are examined.

1028 Sorel, Claudette. "Equal Opportunity for Women Pianists." Music Journal 26:41, March 1968.
Briefly traces the history of women pianists from Nannerl Mozart to the 1960's. The conclusion is that women are still not prominent on the concert scene for reasons unrelated to talent. Women were not encouraged to make careers in music, the large number of women who attended concerts lead to idolization of male performers, and the belief that women were not strong enough to fully utilize the tonal capabilities of the piano, according to Sorel.

1029 _____. Mind Your Musical Manners, Off and On Stage. New York: Marks Music Corp., 1972.
This is a stage etiquette handbook which covers such items as appropriate concert attire for both men and women.

1030 Sorrels, Rosalie. What, Woman, and Who, Myself, I Am: An Anthology of Songs and Poetry of Women's

Experience. Sonoma, Calif.: Wooden Shoe, 1974.
Includes melodies with chord symbols.

1031 Spaeth, Sigmund Gottfried. The Importance of Music. New York: Fleet Pub. Corp., 1963.
Among these short essays are references to many women musicians.

1032 Speaks, C. P. "Women's Liberation: From Cosí Fan Tutte to Falstaff!" Your Music Cue 7(7):3-7, 1971.

1033 Sperry, Gale L. "Women Are Here to Stay." Instrumentalist 8:30-31, March 1954.
Sperry was the director of marching bands at the University of Minnesota during 1954. His experiences with women bands have led him to conclude that there should be separate bands for men and women. Also, he felt that shows written for the women's band should be ladylike and the girls should have feminine uniforms.

1034 Spiegel, B. "Musical Nuns; Diocesan Teachers Symphony of Pittsburgh." Look 27:45-48, March 12, 1963.
Sixty nuns made up the Diocesan Teachers Symphony of Pittsburgh.

1035 Stambler, Irwin, and Landon, Grelun. Golden Guitars; The Story of Country Music. New York: Four Winds Press, 1971.
This history of country music has many women in its pages, such as Loretta Lynn and Bobbie Gentry.

1036 Starkie, Walter. "Jean of the Singing Ritchies." Saturday Review 43:56, April 16, 1960.
Jean Ritchie is a member of the folk-singing Ritchies of Kentucky. This is a review of her recording "Carols of All Seasons."

1037 Starr, Susan. "The Prejudice Against Women." Music Journal 32:14, March 1974.
Ms. Starr, a concert pianist, described the prejudice she and other women in the field have faced.

1038 "The State of the Profession." College Music Symposium 14:164-170, 1974.

A report from the 16th meeting of the College Music Symposium which examined the role of the female music student and some the reasons behind sex discrimination in hiring after college graduation.

1039 "Statistics in Music." School Musician 45:56, June-July 1974.
Some statistics of women in the music field during 1974 are as follows: 80 per cent of elementary school music teachers are women while only 27 per cent of them teach in high school.

1040 Steane, J. B. The Grand Tradition; Seventy Years of Singing on Record. New York: Charles Scribner's Sons, 1974.
Covers opera singers from the pre-electrical recording period in 1900 to the prolific recording period of the 1970's. A number of American women, such as Leontyne Price and Beverly Sills, are included in the discussion of recorded operas.

1041 Stern, K. "Theatre of Bel Canto." Opera News 40: 13: February 28, 1976.
Maria Felicia Malibran is the opera singer discussed in relation to the bel canto style of singing.

1042 Sterrett, N. "The Female of the Species." Musical Opinion 86:677, August, 1963.
Concerns choirs and their training.

1043 Sterritt, David. "Fanny: Rock Music's Only All-Girl Team." Christian Science Monitor 65:14, June 8, 1973.
This rock group consists of four girls who have the qualities to achieve success. In an interview they discuss the discrimination they feel because they don't have any males in their band. People are skeptical about the sound an all-girl rock group will produce, and they usually attend these concerts only out of curiosity.

1044 Stevens, E. M. "The Influence of Nadia Boulanger on Composition in the United States; A Study of Piano Solo Works by Her American Students." Mus. A.D. dissertation, Boston University, 1975.

1045 Stevenson, Florence. "One-Woman Show." Opera News

28:26-27, March 7, 1964.
Interview with Rose Landver, a singer and teacher from Germany. She came to the United States in 1939 and has been directing operatic acting.

1046 Stevenson, Janet. <u>Marian Anderson: Singing to the World</u>. Chicago: Encyclopaedia Britannica Press, 1963.
A biography of this black woman who became a famous opera singer.

1047 Stewart-Baxter, Derrick. "Blues & Views (Blues Singers)." <u>Jazz Journal</u> 21:16, September 1968.
This writer answered critics who felt that he had over-emphasized the part women have played in jazz. He argued that female blues singers evolved from Vaudeville and that Mamie Smith recorded the first blues song: "Crazy Blues." He named other female blues performers who have contributed to the field.

1048 _____. "Blues & Views--Make Way for the Ladies." <u>Jazz Journal</u> 23:23, February 1970.
Mr. Stewart-Baxter admitted that he was partial to women blues singers and felt that they have been ignored by most writers. Names like Bessie Smith and Ma Rainey were exceptions. He reviewed a new album recorded by several lesser-known blues singers and gave it a high rating.

1049 Stickney, Doris. "A Service for Choir Mothers." <u>Journal of Church Music</u> 11:9-11, November 1969.
An experiment in having the mothers of children in the choirs go through a rehearsal as if they were in the children's choir themselves. This was done to increase the mothers' awareness of the difficulty children have doing all the things adults feel are easy, such as proceeding down the aisle while singing.

1050 Stoddard, Hope. "As the Conductor Sees It." <u>Instrumental Musician</u> 48:10, September 1949.

1051 _____. <u>Famous American Women</u>. New York: Crowell, 1970.
Includes bibliographies of some American women musicians.

1052 _____. "Fine Musicianship Knows No Sex." Independent Woman 26:316, November 1947.

1053 _____. "Ladies of the Symphony." Instrumental Musician 51:24, May 1953.

1054 Stravinsky, Theodore. Catherine & Igor Stravinsky; A Family Album. London: Boosey & Hawkes, 1973.
The third section of this work covers the years Stravinsky spent in the United States (1939-1971). Written by his son, this biography contains pictures of the family through the years. It gives some indication of Catherine Stravinsky's influence on her husband during his life in music.

1055 "Striking New Concert Gowns of Leading Singers." Etude 60:296, May 1942.
Six costumes are modeled by well-known women singers such as Risë Stevens and Lily Pons.

1056 "Sugar and Spice." Metronome 72:20-23, December 1956.
Female jazz singers are discussed.

1057 "Supreme Sopranos." Time 78:47-48, December 8, 1961.
Sketches of the careers of six of the top sopranos who have sung at the Metropolitan Opera. They are Joan Sutherland, Maria Callas, Renata Tebaldi, Eileen Farrell, Birgit Nilsson, and Leontyne Price.

1058 "Supremes Are Tops." Ebony 21:152-154, August 1966.
A chronicle of the trio which sang their way to success in popular music. They became stars in 1965 when five of their recordings sold more than one million copies each.

1059 "Supremes Make It Big." Ebony 20:80, 1965.
This successful trio from Detroit consists of Diana Ross, Florence Ballard, and Mary Wilson.

1060 Surge, Frank. Singers of the Blues. Minneapolis: Lerner Publications, 1969.
Seventeen musicians who had an influence on the development of the blues are included.

1061 Sutherland, Joan. "Singing in a Tree." Seventeen 24: 164, September 1965.
    Opera is the subject of this discussion by Joan Sutherland.

1062 Sutton, Horace. "Tours for Divas." Saturday Review 37:35-36, September 4, 1954.
    Mary Crennan, transportation manager of Columbia Artists Management, relates some of the eccentricities of traveling that artists such as Lily Pons require.

1063 "Sweet Nancy." Life 60:53, June 24, 1966.
    Nancy Wilson is a black night club singer who has gained popularity in jazz and rock.

1064 "Swingin' Aretha." Ebony 19:85, March 1964.
    Aretha Franklin is known for her "pure gospel" sound in her blues singing. The story of her successful career is told.

1065 Swinyard, L. "Female Quiristers [sic]." Musical Opinion 98:335-336, April 1975.
    An editorial on the discrimination women face in singing in churches. The Women's Liberation movement is helping women to gain more acceptance in this area.

1066 "Symphony Goes Co-ed." Newsweek 22:86, December 6, 1943.
    Statistics showing the increasing number of women in some major symphony orchestras of the nation.

1067 "TV Glam Sparks Femme Orchs." Variety 188:37, December 3, 1952.

1068 "Talk with the Star." Newsweek 59:85, March 26, 1962.
    An interview with the singer-actress Diahann Carroll.

1069 Tallmadge, William H. "Dr. Watts and Mahalia Jackson--the Development, Decline, and Survival of a Folk Style in America." Ethnomusicology 5(2):95-99, 1961.
    The style of "long-meter" or "Dr. Watts" was practiced by American Negroes almost a century

after the custom of "lining-out" the Psalms in white churches was discontinued. The gospel music of Mahalia Jackson is examined in relation to the "Dr. Watts" method.

1070 Tanner, Paul, and Gerow, Maurice. <u>A Study of Jazz</u>. 2nd ed. Dubuque, Iowa: W. C. Brown, 1973.
Ma Rainey, Billie Holiday, and Bessie Smith are three jazz singers whose styles are examined in this work.

1071 Tassin, Myron, and Henderson, Jerry. <u>Fifty Years at the Grand Ole Opry</u>. Gretna, La.: Pelican Pub. Co., 1975.
A pictorial history of country music in Nashville. Women have always been part of the Grand Ole Opry program.

1072 Terkel, Studs. <u>Giants of Jazz</u>. New York: Thomas Y. Crowell Co., 1957.
A chapter is devoted to each of these great women of jazz: Bessie Smith and Billie Holiday.

1073 Teyte, Maggie. <u>Star on the Door</u>. London: Putnam, 1963.
An autobiography of this English singer which details her rise and fall in popularity with the American public.

1074 "They Love That Boy-Girl Sound; More & More Duos Jam Rosters." <u>Billboard</u> 70:4, May 12, 1958.
The rock and roll field is brimming with male-female singing teams.

1075 "Third Annual Music-Record Poll; The Year's Top Selling Female Vocalists over Retail Counters." <u>Billboard</u> 61:13, January 1, 1949.
Includes the singers Peggy Lee, Doris Day, and Dinah Shore.

1076 Thomas, C. W. "Three Negroes Receive 1964 Presidential Freedom Medal." <u>Negro History Bulletin</u> 28:58-59, December 1964.

1077 Thomas, D. "With a Song in Her Heart." <u>Independent Woman</u> 29:40-41, February 1950.
Concerns American folk songs.

1078 Thomas, Tony. Harry Warren and the Hollywood Musical. Secaucus, N.J.: Citadel Press, 1975.
   Almost every page contains photographs of the actors and actresses for whom Warren composed music.

1079 Thompson, Helen Mulford. A Handbook for Symphony Orchestra Women's Associations. Vienna, Va.: American Symphony Orchestra League, 1963.
   A guide for the formation of women's auxiliary organizations and their activities.

1080 Thompson, Thomas. "Almost Nobody's As Classy As Sassy." Life 72:27, June 16, 1972.
   A review of the singing style of Sarah Vaughan as it has developed since she entered Harlem's Apollo Theatre amateur contest at the age of eighteen.

1081 Thomson, Virgil. American Music Since 1910. New York: Holt, Rinehart and Winston, 1971.
   Nadia Boulanger (a famous teacher of Americans) and Peggy Glanville-Hicks (a composer) are the major women musicians treated in this work, but significant biographical information is provided for four other women: Ruth Crawford, Lucia Clugoszewski, Vivian Fine, and Louise Talma.

1082 _____. "Greatest Music Teacher at Seventy-Five." New York Times Magazine February 4, 1962, p. 24.
   Nadia Boulanger has had a great influence on many American musicians although her home has usually been in Paris. Among her famous students are Aaron Copland, Peggy Glanville-Hicks and Louise Talma. In addition to her teaching, she conducted the New York Philharmonic in four concerts during 1962 at the age of seventy-five.

1083 _____. The Musical Scene. New York: Greenwood Press, 1968, c1945.
   Essays and reviews which appeared in the New York Herald Tribune from 1940-1944. Included in the reviews were many concerts by famous women such as Marian Anderson.

1084 Tick, Judith. "Why Have There Been No Great Women Composers?: Or Notes on the Score of Sexual Aesthetics." Instrumental Musician 74:6, July 1975.

1085 Tiegel, E. "Pop Gospel Not of U.S. --Mahalia."
Billboard 75:1, September 28, 1963.
Mahalia Jackson's popular music is discussed.

1086 "Tina Turns On." Life 69:57-61, December 18, 1970.
A review of the singer Tina Turner.

1087 "To Europe and the Holy Land with Mahalia Jackson."
Ebony 16:44, October 1961.
Excerpts from this gospel singer's diary of her trip to Israel detailing her feelings about the concerts she gave along the way.

1088 Tobias, Tobi. Marian Anderson. New York: Crowell, 1972.
A biography of this Negro concert singer written for young people.

1089 Todd, Arthur. "Leontyne Price; Voice of the Century."
Musical America 82:12-15, January 1962.
Examination of this black singer's career in opera.

1090 "Top Bonanzas: Music." Vogue 165:96-97, June 1975.
The conductor Sarah Caldwell received a brief review in this collection of important artists.

1091 "Top Female Vocalists of the Year." Billboard 62:21, October 7, 1950 Suppl.

1092 Tormé, Mel. The Other Side of the Rainbow with Judy Garland on the Dawn Patrol. New York: W. Morrow, 1970.
The story of this singer-entertainer's life, emphasizing her television shows.

1093 Trachter, Ira. "Females' Emergence as Writer/Singer to Persist." Billboard 84:3, January 8, 1972.
It appears that women are making an impact in the music industry as artists and writers. Carole King, Aretha Franklin, and Helen Reddy are examples of musicians who have been able to successfully compete with men.

1094 Traubel, Helen. St. Louis Woman. New York: Duell, Sloan and Pearce, 1959.
Biography of the American opera singer Helen Traubel and the story of her concerts in America and around the world.

1095 Truman, Margaret. "Triumph of Marian Anderson." McCalls 103:114, April 1976.
    Excerpt from Women of Courage which includes Marian Anderson who started a political and racial uproar in 1939 when she was scheduled to sing in Constitution Hall in Washington, D.C. No Negro had sung there before and she was not permitted to sing there either.

1096 _____. Women of Courage. West Caldwell, N.J.: W. Morrow, 1976.
    Consists of selected women who showed remarkable courage in Margaret Truman's opinion. Marian Anderson is the black woman who was denied permission to give a concert in Washington's Constitution Hall because of her race.

1097 Tucker, B. "What Makes Women's Associations Run?" American Symphony Orchestra League Newsletter 24(2):5-7, 1973.

1098 "Two Coloured Prima Donnas." Record Research 67:5, April 1965.

1099 "Two First 'First Ladies' in Music Education." Triangle 65(2):12-14, 1971.
    Celia Mae Bryant was the president of the Music Teachers National Association and Frances M. Andrews was president of the Music Educators National Conference in 1971. Both were the first women to be elected president of their respective organizations. Short biographies were given as well as their views on music.

1100 "Two Gatherings." New Yorker 50:31-32, March 25, 1974.
    An examination of Aretha Franklin's style of singing at a New York Apollo Theatre performance.

1101 "Typical Teacher Is Virtuoso." School Musician 40:87, August-September 1968.
    A prototype of a typical private music teacher emerged from a nationwide survey by the Music Teachers National Association. Eighty per cent were women, married, age 36-55, and teaching piano.

1102 Ulanov, Barry. A History of Jazz in America. New

York: Viking Press, 1957, c1952.
References to women who were important in the development of jazz included Bessie Smith, Lil Hardin, and Billie Holiday.

1103 _____. "Women in Jazz: Do They Belong?" Down Beat 25:17, January 9, 1958.
Ulanov attempts to answer the question, "Is there a place for women in jazz strictly on a merit basis?" Discrimination against women instrumentalists in jazz groups is common even though there are some all-female groups.

1104 Ulrich, Homer. Famous Women Singers. New York: Dodd, Mead, 1953.
Biographies of women who became famous for their voices. Written for young people.

1105 "Unadorned Femme Singles Rare Now; Vogue to Boy Backgrounders on Rise." Variety 197:50, January 26, 1955.

1106 "Unique Organization: Nuns' Band at De Paul University." Etude 63:196, April 1945.
This was possibly the first band composed entirely of nuns. Pictures and information about the organization were given.

1107 Uselton, R. A. "Opera Singers As Film Stars: Many Recruited, Few Big at B.O." Variety 249:11, January 3, 1968.

1108 Valentry, Duane. "The Gals Are Singing." Music Journal 14:43-45, October 1956.
The rural women of the Indiana Home Demonstration Clubs have joined their voices in active choral groups across the state. Much enthusiasm has been shown for learning to sing.

1109 Van de Vate, Nancy. "The American Woman Composer: Some Sour Notes." High Fidelity/Musical America 25:MA18-19, June 1975.
Ms. Van de Vate, a composer and president of the Southeastern Composers League, related the problems women face in attaining even modest recognition. One of the purposes of the recently formed League of Women Composers is to try to provide better opportunities for women.

1110 _____. "Every Good Boy (Composer) Does Fine (Recordings)." American Symphony Orchestra League Newsletter 24(6):11-13, 1973-1974.
    A discussion of the discrimination women composers face.

1111 Vance, Marcia. "A Girl (!) Record Collector?" Bim Bam Boom August-September 1974, pp. 67-68.

1112 Vehanen, Kosti. Marian Anderson; A Portrait. Westport, Conn.: Greenwood Press, 1970, c1941.
    This book covers the concert life of the American black singer Marian Anderson. Her childhood is omitted. Anderson toured in Europe and later became a regular performer in the New York Metropolitan Opera.

1113 Verrill, A. "Rock 'Girl Tramps' Grim Film Focus." Variety 259:1, July 8, 1970.

1114 "Vocalise; How Long Can a Soprano Practice without Infringing on the Rights of Her Neighbors?" Musical America 72:11, July 1952.
    A court case which was decided in favor of the plaintiffs who resided in the apartment next to the soprano.

1115 "Voice Like a Banner Flying." Time 77:58, March 10, 1961.
    Leontyne Price's great operatic voice is examined.

1116 Wagenknecht, Edward Charles. Seven Daughters of the Theater. Norman: University of Oklahoma, 1964.
    Mary Garden and Jenny Lind are discussed in this work.

1117 Wagner, Alan. Prima Donnas and Other Wild Beasts. Larchmont, N.Y.: Argonaut Books, 1961.
    Anecdotes about musicians make up this work.

1118 Walsh, A. "Scrubbers--the Facts." Melody Maker 41:10-11, December 10, 1966.
    Concerns female popular music fans.

1119 Walsh, J. "Favorite Pioneer Recording Artists and Some Forgotten Woman Singers." Hobbies 57:24-26, April 1952.

1120 _____. "That Girl Quartet and Other Women's Groups." Hobbies 77:37, February 1973.

1121 Walton, Ortiz. Music: Black, White & Blue; A Sociological Survey of the Use and Misuse of Afro-American Music. New York: W. Morrow, 1972.
   The discrimination in orchestral hiring suffered by blacks and women has been very similar. Walton feels that although the women's liberation movement has managed to promote the hiring of minorities in orchestras, it often results in women receiving the positions instead of blacks.

1122 Warren, Dale. "The Disappearing Contralto." American Record Guide 27:276-279, December 1960.
   Sopranos seem to be the singers always in the spotlight and lower registers are seldom acclaimed. Various roles that contraltos have sung are discussed.

1123 Warren, L. "How Do Male Opera Stars Make It Against the Glittering Prima Donna?" Variety 205:76, December 12, 1956.

1124 Waters, Ethel, and Samuels, Charles. His Eye Is on the Sparrow; An Autobiography. Garden City, N.Y.: Doubleday, 1951.
   The autobiography of this Negro singer and entertainer. Waters performed chiefly in New York theaters.

1125 _____. To Me It's Wonderful. New York: Harper & Row, 1972.
   Memories of Ethel Waters are related in this autobiography. Her life as a singer-entertainer includes acting on Broadway as well as singing in the Billy Graham crusades.

1126 Weinstock, Herbert. "Maria, Renata, Zinka: And Leonora." Saturday Review 40:56-57, April 13, 1957.
   Maria Callas, Zinka Milanov, and Renata Tebaldi are three sopranos reviewed in this article which discusses specific recordings each has made.

1127 Weller, Sheila. "Carla Bley ... and All Her Jazz." Ms. 4:35-37, August 1975.
   This is an interview with Carla Bley, who is pos-

sibly the first woman to make a career as a jazz composer.

1128 West, Stephen. "Concerning the Contralto." Etude 64:315-316, June 1946.
   Evelyn MacGregor is interviewed and gives her opinions on the best way to train and preserve a good contralto voice.

1129 _____. "What About the Woman Violinist?" Etude 65:485-486, September 1947.
   Evelyn (Mrs. Phil) Spitalny has been the concertmaster and soloist on the CBS radio program "Hour of Charm" for years. She is a member of Phil Spitalny's all-girl orchestra. She expressed her feelings about the needs of women violinists.

1130 "What Ever Happened to Rubina Flake?" Time 105: 62-63, Mary 12, 1975.
   Roberta Flack is the singer discussed.

1131 White, Jackie. "4 Women of Calibre." Country Music July 1974, pp. 62-66.

1132 "Wife Begins at Forty-Plus." Etude 66:135, March 1948.
   A grandmother tells how she and her husband were inspired to begin music lessons in their later years after reading an article in Etude.

1133 Wilgus, D. K. "On the Record." Kentucky Folklore Record 8(3):111-112, 1962.
   Jean Ritchie talks about the origins of hillbilly music.

1134 Wilkinson, G. "Oscar, Ella, and Louis." Jazz Journal 9:1, June 1956.
   Ella Fitzgerald is discussed in this article on jazz.

1135 Williams, B. "Female Country Acts Succeed in 8 Ratio." Billboard 87:4, April 12, 1975.
   "The ratio of female country singers on the Billboard country chart this week is almost exactly proportionate to the number of female artists on the major labels, a study shows."

1136 _____. "Ladies in the Driver's Seat." Billboard 80:54-55, October 19, 1968 Suppl.
Discussion of women in the music industry.

1137 _____. "The Ladies of Nashville." Billboard 82: CM41, October 17, 1970.
The country music empire of Nashville has many women as heads of various recording and managing businesses. Short career sketches plus photographs of seven successful ladies are included.

1138 _____. "Nashville Battle Scene of Sexes; Gal Writers Click." Billboard 81:83, May 19, 1969.

1139 Williams, Martin T. The Art of Jazz; Essays on the Nature and Development of Jazz. New York: Oxford University Press, 1959.
Two chapters are devoted to successful women in jazz: Bessie Smith and Billie Holiday.

1140 _____. "Ella and Others." Saturday Review 47:51, November 28, 1964.
A review of the popular singing style of Ella Fitzgerald plus a number of others such as Peggy Lee and Nancy Wilson.

1141 _____. Jazz Masters of New Orleans. New York: Macmillan, 1967.
Bessie Smith, Ma Rainey, and Lil Hardin are among the jazz musicians who had their roots in New Orleans.

1142 _____. Jazz Panorama, from the Pages of the Jazz Review. New York: Collier Books, 1967, c1962.
The recordings of Billie Holiday are reviewed in one section devoted to her music.

1143 _____. The Jazz Tradition. New York: Oxford University Press, 1970.
One woman is discussed in this collection of essays. Chapter 6 is "Billy Holiday: Actress without an Act."

1144 _____. Where's the Melody? A Listener's Introduction to Jazz. Rev. ed. New York: Pantheon Books, 1969.

This examination of jazz includes the women musicians Billie Holiday and Bessie Smith.

1145 Williams, Paul. Outlaw Blues: A Book of Rock Music. New York: E. P. Dutton, 1969.
Williams started the rock and roll magazine Crawdaddy. Most of the material in the book first appeared in his magazine. Grace Slick of the Jefferson Airplane is the most prominent woman in this collection of writings.

1146 Williams, Richard. "Who Were the Women [That] Composers Have Loved." House Beautiful 87:85, June 1945.
Discussion of the women in the lives of famous musicians.

1147 Willis, Ellen. "But Now I'm Gonna Move." New Yorker 47:168, October 23, 1971.
Discussion of the women's movement in rock music. The rock era began as a strictly masculine enterprise. The performers and almost everyone in the concert and recording business was male. However, women's liberation resulted in more opportunities offered to women.

1148 _____. "Rock, etc.; Roseland Nation." New Yorker 49:111-223, October 29, 1973.
The Pointer Sisters, a quartet of black women, are discussed in this article.

1149 Wilmer, Valerie. Jazz People. London: Allison & Busby, 1970.
Only brief references are made to the following women singers: Nina Simone, Ella Fitzgerald, and Billie Holiday.

1150 Wilson, T. "Handbags in the Band Wagon." Melody Maker 43:11, March 9, 1968.
Girls who play in popular combos are discussed.

1151 Winstone, E. "Attention Please, Those Girl Singers." Melody Maker 30:2, August 21, 1954.
Advice is given to women who are aspiring to be vocalists.

1152 Wisneski, Herbert. Maria Callas; The Art behind the

Legend. New York: Doubleday, 1975.
A biography of the opera soprano Maria Callas.

1153 Wodehouse, P. G., and Golton, G. R. Bring on the Girls! New York: Simon and Schuster, 1954.

1154 "Woman's Philharmonic Orchestra." Violins 10:39, January 1949.

1155 "A Woman's Touch in Music." Variety 275:58, May 15, 1974.

1156 "Women and Musical Instruments." Music Journal 27: 93, April 1969.
More adult women are learning or continuing to play musical instruments lately. According to this article, a hobby of this type can be very beneficial psychologically.

1157 "Women Composers: En Route; Results of an Editorial Survey." High Fidelity/Musical America 25:MA21, June 1975.
A survey of the percentage of women composition students and faculty in major North American conservatories and universities. Also, the results of a survey in which five major U.S. orchestras were asked to list works written by women that they had performed during the past ten years.

1158 "Women Conductors." Instrumental Musician 57:39, January 1959.

1159 "Women Have Hard Way to Go in Country: Rutledge." Billboard 86:46, January 12, 1974.
Virginia Rutledge relates her problems in obtaining bookings for women in Las Vegas. She has managed to place two country singers during 1973: Judy Lynn and Tanya Tucker.

1160 "Women in Big 10 Marching Bands." School Musician 45:58-59, December 1973.
A survey of women band members in universities which are part of the Big Ten Conference, such as Ohio State and Michigan. Some of these bands were all-male until a short time before 1973.

1161 "Women in Music." Pan Pipes 67:2-3, January 1975.

"Encounters with women in music, an illustrated lecture series" was held at California State University, Los Angeles. The women performers and composers who were part of this series are listed.

1162 "Women in Orchestras." *Instrumental Musician* 63:20, November 1964.

1163 "Women Wanted for Marine Band." *Musician* 48:114, October 1943.
The Marine Corp Women's Reserve Band at Camp Lejeune, North Carolina, will fill in for male Marines who will be released for combat duty in the war.

1164 "Womenfolk." *Ebony* 19:182-185, June 1964.
"All-girl folk singing quintet catches fancy of West Coast night club audience." The group has recorded two albums: "We Give a Hoot" and "Womenfolk."

1165 "Women's Association and Composers." *American Symphony Orchestra League Newsletter* 7:7, June 1956.

1166 "Women's Associations--Fund Raising Projects." *American Symphony Orchestra League Newsletter* 7:8-9, June 1956.

1167 "Women's Auxiliaries--Widen Your Local's Scope." *Instrumental Musician* 63:8, June 1965.

1168 "Women's Lib Hits Piano Travelers Association." *Music Trades* 119:48, September 1971.

1169 "Women's Lib in New York." *Black Perspective in Music* 2(1):107, 1974.
An all-woman jazz band (believed to be the first in twenty-five years) performed November 4, 1973, at the Calvert Extra Sunday Concerts at the Jazz Museum in New York. This historical sextet included Carline Ray, Julie Gardner, and Jean Davis.

1170 "Works by Women Composers in New Recording." *Music Clubs Magazine* 50(4):9, 1971; 51(3):31, 1972.

1171 Wren, Christopher S. "Little Peggy Hits the Big

Time." Look 27:Z4, October 22, 1963.
Story of a teenage girl who was discovered singing at a church wedding and was promoted as a popular singer.

1172 Wright, G. "Career Opportunities for the Young Woman Graduate." School Musician 46:41, June-July 1975.
Opportunity as a school band director is suggested for women.

1173 Wylie, Evan McLeod. "I Can't Stop Singing." Saturday Evening Post 232:19, December 5, 1959.
An interview with the gospel singer Mahalia Jackson who tells of her lifetime of singing the songs of God.

1174 "You Won't Have 'Lady Musicians' To Kick Around Much Longer." Music Educators Journal 59:inside front cover, September 1972.
A challenge to women to try harder to infiltrate all ranks of the music field. Statistics are given showing that women are greatly outnumbered in administrative areas, performance (except singers), and teaching (except elementary levels).

1175 "Your Favorite Contraltos." Hobbies 49:22, January; 25-26, February; 50:17, March 1945.

1176 Zimmermann, G. "Taylor Girls: Nitty Gritty Twins." Look 33:68, March 4, 1969.
Rae and Kay Taylor worked with the rock group the Nitty Gritty Dirt Band.

GENERAL HISTORY

1177 American Music Conference. "The Women of Music." Music Journal 30:9-24, January 1972.
    A good general history of women in music, including the contributions of Americans.

1178 Ayars, Christine Merrick. Contributions to the Art of Music in America by the Music Industries of Boston, 1640-1936. New York: Johnson Reprint Corp., 1969, c1937.
    Detailed history of music publishers and instrument makers in Boston. The section on "The Arthur P. Schmidt Co." lists several prominent American women composers, including Mrs. H. H. A. Beach and Marion Bauer, pp. 38-41.

1179 Barnes, Edwin Ninyon Chaloner. American Music; From Plymouth Rock to Tin Pan Alley. Washington, D.C.: Music Education Pub., 1936.
    "A resumé of three centuries of American music."

1180 ———. American Women in Creative Music: Tuning In on American Music. Washington, D.C.: Music Education Pub., 1936.
    Examines the place of American women in music.

1181 Bauer, Marion, and Peyser, Ethel. Music Through the Ages; A Narrative for Student and Layman. 3rd ed. New York: G. P. Putnam's Sons, 1967.
    A section within the "Music in America" chapter is devoted to Mrs. H. H. A. Beach and to other Americans.

1182 Bean, Helen J. "Women in the Music House." American Music Teacher 6:4, March-April 1957.

1183 Birge, Edward Bailey. History of Public School Mu-

General History

sic in the United States. Washington, D.C.: Music Educators National Conference, 1966.
   Birge's history traces music education from the singing schools to the 1920's. Music training was provided to women and they became quite active in the Music Teachers' Associations.

1184 Blum, Daniel C. A Pictorial Treasury of Opera in America. New York: Greenberg, 1954.
   This book is a good pictorial history of American opera from the 1700's to the 1950's. Women performers are pictured in the majority of the photographs.

1185 Borroff, Edith. "Woman Composers: Reminiscence and History." College Music Symposium 15:26-33, 1975.
   Ms. Borroff was rejected as a composition student at the Oberlin Conservatory in 1944 because women were not considered seriously in the composition field at that time. She presents a survey of women composers through the ages.

1186 Britain, Radie. "Musical Composition--A New World for Women." Instrumentalist 25:55-56, November 1970.
   Brief history of women composers through the past few centuries. The author feels that women are beginning to receive equal opportunities in the field of music composition during the 1970's. The article provides some background into the social conditions of past cultures which held back the musical education of women.

1187 Brockway, Wallace, and Weinstock, Herbert. The World of Opera; The Story of Its Development and the Lore of Its Performances. New York: Modern Library, 1966.

1188 Burns, Don. "The Distaff'd Composers." Music Journal 32:16, March 1974.
   A brief history of the discrimination women composers have faced throughout history.

1189 Burton, Jack. The Blue Book of Broadway Musicals. Watkins Glen, N.Y.: Century House, 1969.
   This anthology of over 1500 productions that have

played on Broadway covers the beginnings through the 1960's. Few women wrote Broadway musicals, but many women singers' names are included in information about the productions.

1190 _____. <u>The Blue Book of Tin Pan Alley; A Human Interest Encyclopedia of American Popular Music.</u> Rev. ed. Watkins Glen, N.Y.: Century House, 1962.

There are a few references to women jazz composers such as Maude Nugent. Unfortunately, the Index of Composers and Lyricists is brief and omits names of many minor jazz musicians discussed in the material; most of the women fall into this category.

1191 Charters, Samuel Barclay. <u>Jazz: New Orleans, 1885-1963; An Index to the Negro Musicians of New Orleans.</u> Rev. ed. New York: Oak Publications, 1963.

1192 Chase, Gilbert. <u>America's Music: From the Pilgrims to the Present.</u> 2nd ed. New York: McGraw-Hill Book Co., 1966.

An extensive account of America's musical history, especially the eighteenth and nineteenth centuries. There are limited references to individual women's contributions.

1193 Cook, Bruce. <u>Listen to the Blues.</u> New York: Scribner's Sons, 1973.

A book about the men and women who sang the blues. Among the profiles of the musicians are such important names as Bessie Smith and Janis Joplin.

1194 Cook, Ida. <u>We Followed Our Stars.</u> London: Hamish Hamilton, 1950.

Correspondence and reminiscences of opera singers.

1195 Cron, Theodore O., and Goldblatt, Burt. <u>Portrait of Carnegie Hall; A Nostalgic Portrait in Pictures and Words of America's Greatest Stage and the Artists Who Performed There.</u> New York: Macmillan, 1966.

History and pictures of many women are included.

General History

1196 Daniels, M. "The Woman Composer of Yesterday and Today." Music Clubs Magazine 39(5):12-13, 1960.

1197 Davis, Ronald L. A History of Opera in the American West. Englewood Cliffs, N.J.: Prentice-Hall, 1965.
This history of opera in the western part of the United States includes a number of references to American divas who participated in these opera productions, such as Leontyne Price.

1198 _____. Opera in Chicago. New York: Appleton-Century, 1966.
Many of the world famous divas have performed in Chicago operas and are discussed in this history.

1199 Drinker, Sophie Lewis. Music and Women: The Story of Women in Their Relation to Music. New York: Coward-McCann, 1948.
This work traces women in the history of music of the world with an examination of the reasons they have not been more prominent in the field.

1200 Eaton, Quaintance. The Miracle of the Met; An Informal History of the Metropolitan Opera, 1883-1967. New York: Meredith Press, 1968.
Chapter 2, "The Women," examines the ladies of society and their dress and conduct as it related to opera attendance from about 1850-1950. The many productions of the Met over the years have utilized the greatest singers in the world. Among them are a significant number of American singers.

1201 _____. Opera Caravan; Adventures of the Metropolitan on Tour, 1883-1956. New York: Farrar, Straus & Cudahy, 1957.
A history of the travels of the Metropolitan Opera along with the roster of singers in the performances. Many American women were among the singers.

1202 Ellingwood, Leonard. The History of American Church Music. New York: Morehouse-Gorham Co., 1953.
A small number of women are included in this history; two are discussed in depth in Appendix C: "Biographies of American Church Musicians."

1203 Elson, Arthur, and Truette, Everette E. *Woman's Work in Music*. Rev. ed. Boston: L. C. Page, 1931.
"An account of her influence on the art, in ancient as well as modern times; a summary of her musical compositions, in the different countries of the civilized world; and an estimate of their rank in comparison with those of men."

1204 Elson, Louis Charles. *The History of American Music*. Rev. ed. New York: Macmillan Co., 1915.
Chapter 15, "American Women in Music," gives a good history of prominent women composers and performers in early America.

1205 _____. *Woman in Music*. New York: University Society, 1918.
This history traces the influence of women on music from ancient times to the 20th century. Chapter 8 is "Women Composers of America."

1206 Engel, Carl. "What Great Music Owes to Women." *Etude* 47:797-798, November 1929.
Mr. Engel examined the great influence women have had on composers of the past. No individual women are discussed, but their general contributions are noted.

1207 Engel, Lehman. *The American Musical Theater*. Rev. ed. New York: Macmillan, 1975.
A history of musicals in America which involved many women singers, actors, and dancers.

1208 Ewen, David. *Complete Book of the American Musical Theater; A Guide to More Than 300 Productions of the American Musical Theater from the Black Crook (1866) to the Present, with Plot, Production History, Stars, Composers, Librettists, and Lyricists*. Rev. ed. New York: Holt, 1959.
Includes many women performers.

1209 _____. *History of Popular Music*. New York: Barnes & Noble, 1961.
A few short references to women are found in the brief survey of popular music in the U.S.

1210 _____. *Music Comes to America*. New York:

General History

Thomas Y. Crowell Co., 1942.
A history of American music which includes women musicians who influenced musical development, such as Jenny Lind and the Women's Symphony Orchestra of California.

1211 _____. New Complete Book of the American Musical Theater. New York: Holt, Rinehart, and Winston, 1970.
Women played a major role as performers in the musical theater, but some were successful librettists, lyricists, and composers. Part 2 of this work includes biographical information on several prominent women in the field.

1212 _____. Panorama of American Popular Music; The Story of Our National Ballads and Folk Songs, the Songs of Tin Pan Alley, Broadway and Hollywood, New Orleans Jazz, Swing, and Symphonic Jazz. Englewood Cliffs, N.J.: Prentice-Hall, 1957.
This book is a comprehensive history of all types of popular music from colonial times to the 1950's. Short references are made to many women singers.

1213 Feather, Leonard G. The Book of Jazz, from Then till Now; A Guide to the Entire Field. Rev. ed. New York: Horizon Press, 1965.
This story of jazz contains little information about the women who were important in the development of jazz. Bessie Smith, however, is included.

1214 Fenwick, George Roy. Singers upon Earth. Vancouver: Copp Clark Pub. Co., 1961.

1215 Galloway, Tod Buchanan. "Noted Women in Musical History." Etude 47:809-810, November 1929.
This composer traces the lives of notable women in music and the influence they have had on the profession. He includes names from the past as well as early twentieth-century musicians.

1216 Gishford, Anthony. Grand Opera; The Story of the World's Leading Opera Houses and Personalities. New York: Viking Press, 1972.
One section concentrates on three prominent American opera houses and their singers: the Metropolitan Opera, New York; the Civic Opera,

Chicago; and the War Memorial House, San Francisco. American sopranos such as Maria Callas are pictured.

1217 Green, Miriam. "Women: From Silence to Song." American Music Teacher 24(1):5-7, 1974.
Traces women composers through music history. Several contemporary American women are discussed briefly, such as Pauline Oliveros, Ludmila Ulehla, and Miriam Gideon.

1218 Green, Stanley. The World of Musical Comedy; The Story of the American Musical Stage as Told Through the Careers of Its Foremost Composers and Lyricists. 3rd ed. South Brunswick, N.J.: A. S. Barnes, 1974.
Women performers in musical comedies are abundant, but few are found among the composers. This book includes much information about individual performances and performers.

1219 Hitchcock, Hugh Wiley. Music in the United States: A Historical Introduction. Englewood Cliffs, N.J.: Prentice-Hall, 1974.
A good background of American music. A few references are made to women musicians and can be located quickly by scanning the index.

1220 Howard, John Tasker. Our American Music; A Comprehensive History from 1620 to the Present. 4th ed. New York: Thomas Y. Crowell, 1965.
An excellent work on the history of America's music which includes information on individual women musicians.

1221 _____ and Bellows, George Kent. A Short History of Music in America. Rev. ed. New York: Thomas Y. Crowell, 1967.
Covers music from the beginnings in America to the 1950's. Women composers as Mrs. H. H. A. Beach, Mary Howe, and Marion Bauer are given the greatest recognition.

1222 Hubbard, William Lines. History of American Music. Toledo: I. Squire, 1908.
Included in the discussion of women musicians is a study of Mrs. H. H. A. Beach who is one of the most prominent early composers.

1223 Johnson, Harold Earle. Symphony Hall, Boston.
Boston: Little, Brown and Co., 1950.
Many women have performed in the Boston Symphony Hall in concerts throughout its history.

1224 Johnson, Helen. "The California Women's Symphony Orchestra; The Story of the Orchestra." Etude 73:11, August 1955.
A history of the California Women's Symphony, earlier known as the Los Angeles Women's Symphony Orchestra. This is the oldest orchestra on the West Coast. Ruth Haroldson was the conductor of this group in 1955.

1225 Kolodin, Irving. The Metropolitan Opera, 1883-1966; A Candid History. 4th ed. New York: A. A. Knopf, 1966.
Many individual American sopranos and contraltos are treated in this history of the New York opera house.

1226 Kubly, Herbert. "Maids of the Stradivarius." Mademoiselle 27:208, September 1948.
An historical look at women violinists of the past. Mary Powell of Illinois (1868-1920) was considered one of the greatest. Many contemporary women violinists are discussed at length.

1227 Lahee, Henry Charles. Annals of Music in America; A Chronological Record of Significant Musical Events, from 1640 to the Present Day, with Comments on the Various Periods into Which the Work Is Divided. New York: AMS Press, 1969, c1922.
Detailed list of significant musical events by year with comments and material on these events. The concert listings include many women, especially as singers.

1228 _____. Famous Singers of To-day and Yesterday. Boston: L. C. Page, 1898.

1229 _____. Grand Opera in America. Boston: L. C. Page, 1901.
A thorough treatment of American opera, with much information on the female singers in these performances.

1230 Lang, Paul Henry. One Hundred Years of Music in

America. New York: G. Schirmer, 1961.
   Covers American musical life from approximately 1861-1961 which was also the first hundred years of the publishing house of G. Schirmer. Many references are made to women in the chapter, "The Plush Era in American Concert Life."

1231 Laufe, Abe. Broadway's greatest musicals. New York: Funk & Wagnalls, 1973.
   Women performers such as Ethel Merman and Mary Martin are included in this comprehensive history of musicals performed in New York City.

1232 Loesser, Arthur. Men, Women and Pianos; A Social History. New York: Simon and Schuster, 1954.
   A number of virtuosi who performed in America are discussed.

1233 Lomax, Alan. The Folk Songs of North America in the English Language. New York: Doubleday, 1960.
   Each of the 317 songs are annotated and the subject matter is predominantly women. Lomax believes that "most of the ballads ... have to do with sexual conflict viewed through feminine eyes ... for whom love and marriage meant gruelling labour, endless childbearing, and subservience."

1234 Madeira, Louis Cephas. Annals of Music in Philadelphia and History of the Musical Fund Society from Its Organization in 1820 to the Year 1858. New York: Da Capo Press, 1973, c1896.
   The musical performances during the period 1820-1858 included a number of women. Chapter 12, "The Age of Song: Sontag and Lind: The Future," examines the concerts of Jenny Lind and Henriette Sontag in Philadelphia.

1235 Mander, Raymond, and Mitchenson, Joe. Musical Comedy; A Story in Pictures. London: Peter Davies, 1969.
   A pictorial history of musical comedies from about 1898 to 1968. Female performers are pictured in most of the photographs.

1236 Marcuse, Maxwell F. Tin Pan Alley in Gaslight; A Saga of the Songs That Made the Gray Nineties "Gay." Watkins Glen, N.Y.: Century House, 1959.

The subject matter of songs of the gaslight era were frequently women, as in "Hello, Ma Baby" and "I'll Take You Home Again Kathleen." Women singers as Bessie Smith were prominent during this period.

1237 Marek, George Richard. The World Treasury of Grand Opera, Its Triumphs, Trials, and Great Personalities. New York: Harper, 1957.
Maria Malibran and Adelina Patti are the two prima donnas most prominently treated in this work. Information on their American performances is given.

1238 Marks, Edward Bennet. They All Had Glamour, from the Swedish Nightingale to the Naked Lady. New York: J. Messner, 1944.
Marks examines the lives of famous people in the arts, particularly music. Among them are many women who gave concerts in America and had some "glamour" in attracting the public. Among those discussed are Jenny Lind, Minnie Hauk and Adelina Patti.

1239 Martin, Deac C. T. Deac Martin's Book of Musical Americana. Englewood Cliffs, N.J.: Prentice-Hall, 1970.
Contains material about women's suffrage and songs such as "Please, Little Suffragette," which implied that men would be dependent upon women for decision-making in the future.

1240 Martinez, Raymond Joseph. Portraits of New Orleans Jazz; Its Peoples and Places. New Orleans: Hope Publications, 1971.
"A rather loose collection of stories, pictures, and little bits of information on New Orleans jazz, its people and places."--Preface. Notes on two women in jazz are included with photographs: Sweet Emma Barrett and Blanche Thomas who are still performing in the 1970's.

1241 Matthews, Thomas. The Splendid Art; A History of the Opera. New York: Crowell-Collier Press, 1970.
Marian Anderson and Leontyne Price are two famous black Americans who are discussed in the

chapter entitled "Several Americans--and One Britten."

1242 Matz, Mary Jane. *Opera: Grand and Not So Grand.* New York: William Morrow, 1966.
Chapter 5, "Singers and Their Careers," gives general information about opera singers of the past and present, male and female.

1243 _____. *Opera Stars in the Sun; Intimate Glimpses of Metropolitan Personalities.* New York: Farrar, Straus & Cudahy, 1955.
Short stories about Metropolitan stars' lives away from the stage. Many American women are included such as Marian Anderson and Roberta Peters.

1244 Mellers, Wilfrid Howard. *Music in a New Found Land: Themes and Developments in the History of American Music.* London: Barrie and Rockcliffe, 1964.
Bessie Smith is the woman musician who receives the most coverage in the chapter "Heterophony and Improvision: The New Orleans Jazz Band and King Oliver; Bessie Smith and the Urban Blues."

1245 Merkling, Frank. *The Golden Horseshoe; The Life and Times of the Metropolitan Opera House.* New York: Viking Press, 1965.
A pictorial history of the New York Metropolitan House from 1883 to the 1960's with many prima donnas being a part of that history.

1246 Murtagh, Rena. "Women in the Arts." *Music Journal* 21:54, October 1963.
An historical background of women in the creative arts with an emphasis on musicians. A good overview of major contributors from various countries during the nineteenth and twentieth centuries.

1247 Pahlen, Kurt. *Great Singers from the Seventeenth Century to the Present Day.* New York: Stein and Day, 1974.
A history of famous opera singers which includes information on a number of American prima donnas such as Marian Anderson and Leontyne Price.

1248 Paul, Elliot. *That Crazy American Music.* Indianapolis: Bobbs-Merrill, 1957.

157   General History

    A light-hearted story of musical development in America including the contributions of such women as Bessie Smith and Jenny Lind.

1249 Peltz, Mary Ellis. Behind the Gold Curtain; The Story of the Metropolitan Opera: 1883-1950. New York: Farrar Straus, 1950.
    A short history of the Metropolitan Opera House including photographs of some of the most distinguished opera stars who performed there. Among them were the American women Lillian Nordica and Helen Traubel.

1250 _____. The Magic of the Opera; A Picture Memoir of the Metropolitan. New York: Praeger, 1960.
    Almost entirely pictures. Prima donnas throughout the Metropolitan's history are included.

1251 Pleasants, Henry. The Great American Popular Singers. London: Gollancz, 1974.
    Half of the twenty-two popular singers treated at length in this work are women such as Billie Holiday, Peggy Lee, Bessie Smith, Judy Garland, and Ethel Merman.

1252 _____. The Great Singers from the Dawn of Opera to Our Own Time. New York: Simon and Schuster, 1966.
    Some of the greatest singers have been women and this book is a thorough history of them. Singers who influenced the American concert scene are examined, from Jenny Lind to Marian Anderson.

1253 Preston, Stuart. Farewell to the Old House; The Metropolitan Opera House 1883-1966. Garden City, N.Y.: Doubleday, 1966.
    Pictures of the old Metropolitan Opera House along with many photographs of singers who have performed there such as Lotte Lehman.

1254 Ritter, Frederic Louis. Music in America. 2nd ed. New York: Johnson Reprint Corp., 1970, c1890.
    Covers the 1620's to the late 1800's. Detailed accounts of women are found in the chapters on operas and oratorios in the major cities.

1255 Rublowsky, John. Black Music in America. New York: Basic Books, 1971.

A history of black music as it evolved from Africa and the slave trade to the jazz of today. Rublowsky's work emphasizes the early period of black music, but includes musicians such as Aretha Franklin of the mid-1900's.

1256 _____. Music in America. New York: Crowell-Collier Press, 1967.
Covers the history of America from the time of the colonies to the 1960's. A few short references are made to women.

1257 Sablosky, Irving L. American Music. Chicago: University of Chicago Press, 1969.
Organized by topics, this work traces the rise of music in America from its beginnings to the 1960's. A few women are included and references to them can be found quickly through the index.

1258 Schaun, George. The Story of Music in America. Annapolis, Md.: Greenberry Pubs., 1965.
An outline of music in America. A few women musicians are mentioned but this source was designed to be brief and therefore contains few details.

1259 Schickel, Richard. The World of Carnegie Hall. New York: Julian Messner, 1960.
Many women have performed on the stage of Carnegie Hall.

1260 Shanet, Howard. Philharmonic: A History of New York's Orchestra. New York: Doubleday, 1975.
Many women were active in the New York Philharmonic's history as orchestra members and as administrators.

1261 Sherman, John K. Music and Maestros; The Story of the Minneapolis Symphony Orchestra. Minneapolis: University of Minnesota Press, 1952.
The history of this orchestra which once had a woman manager, Mrs. Carlyle Scott. This orchestra had a woman soloist at its first concert and has had a history of including women in its performances.

1262 Slonimsky, Nicolas. A Thing or Two about Music. Westport, Conn.: Greenwood Press, 1972, c1948.
Anecdotes drawn from newspapers and music

journals as far back as 1784 including many about well-known women in music.

1263 Smith, Cecil Michener. Musical Comedy in America. Theatre Arts Books, 1950.
Women as performers in musical comedies are discussed throughout the book.

1264 _____. "Singers of Songs." Theatre Arts 31:37-40, April 1947.
Outstanding women singers are analyzed. For example, Lotte Lehmann's long operatic career in Austria and the U.S. is related.

1265 _____. Worlds of Music. Philadelphia: J. B. Lippincott, 1952.
This work is divided into sections such as "The Performer's World" and "The World of Opera" which contains short references to women musicians.

1266 Spaeth, Sigmund. A History of Popular Music in America. New York: Random House, 1948.
Spaeth's history is an excellent detailed source for the study of American popular music from the time of "Yankee Doodle" until the 1940's. Many women are included, but most references are quite brief.

1267 Stedman, Jane W. "If the Tights Fit; Women Playing Men's Roles, and Vice Versa." Opera News 31:6-7, January 7, 1967.
An historical sketch of actresses and opera singers who have played the parts of men on stage.

1268 Swan, Howard. Music in the Southwest, 1825-1950. San Marino, Calif.: Huntington Library, 1952.
Covers music in the mining camps, churches, and schools. The beginning of the Women's Symphony Orchestra of Southern California in 1893 is noted.

1269 Winsor, Justin. The Memorial History of Boston, Including Suffolk County, Massachusetts, 1630-1880. 4 vols. Boston: J. R. Osgood, 1880-1881.
Volume 4, Chapter 7 is "The History of Music in Boston" during the 1880's. Describes the increasing role of women singers as soloists in the oratorio and other concerts.

1270 Zanzig, Augustus Delafield. Music in American Life; Present & Future. Washington, D.C.: McGrath Pub. Co. & National Recreation and Park Association, 1973, c1932.

    This survey of amateur music in America includes discussion of glee clubs for both sexes. Community and school performances are emphasized in this book.

1271 Zeschin, Robert. "Ladies of the Libretto." Opera News 36:26-29, March 18, 1972.

    Sketches of various ladies who have composed opera librettos through the centuries, such as the American poetess Edna St. Vincent Millay.

6

BIBLIOGRAPHIES, DICTIONARIES, AND INDEXES

1272 American Society of Composers, Authors and Publishers. The ASCAP Biographical Dictionary of Composers, Authors and Publishers. 3rd ed. New York: American Society of Composers, Authors and Publishers, 1966.

1273 Baxter, Clairce Howard, and Polk, Videt. Gospel Song Writers Biography. Dallas: Stamps-Baxter Music, 1971.
    Short biographies and photographs of men and women who composed gospel songs.

1274 Bio-Bibliographical Index of Musicians in the United States of America from Colonial Times. 2nd ed. Washington, D.C.: Pan-American Union, Music Sections, 1956.

1275 Burnsworth, Charles Carl. Choral Music for Women's Voices: An Annotated Bibliography of Recommended Works. Metuchen, N.J.: Scarecrow Press, 1968.
    A short history of women in musical performance precedes the annotated bibliography of women's choral music.

1276 Claghorn, Charles Eugene. Biographical Dictionary of American Music. West Nyack, N.Y.: Parker Pub. Co., 1973.
    Contains 5,200 short biographies of American musicians of all forms of music.

1277 Colbert, Warren E. Who Wrote That Song?; or, Who in the Hell Is J. Fred Coots? New York: Revisional Press, 1975.
    "An informal survey of American popular songs and their composers." This work concentrates on the men and women composers of the most popular songs rather than on the performers.

1278 Davidson, Gladys. <u>Opera Biographies</u>. London: Werner Laurie, 1955.
   A representative sampling of opera singers of the past and present. Few American women are included, but there are biographies of many Europeans who performed in the U.S.

1279 _____. <u>A Treasury of Opera Biography</u>. New York: Citadel Press, 1955.
   Biographies of opera singers which include a number of American women.

1280 <u>Directory of American Women Composers</u>. 1st ed. Chicago: National Federation of Music Clubs, 1970.
   Lists over 600 women of the past and the present who have composed music in America.

1281 Drinker, Sophie Lewis. "Music for Women's Choruses --Sacred Song." <u>Music Clubs Magazine</u> 29:13, June 1950.

1282 _____. "Music for Women's Choruses--Secular." <u>Music Clubs Magazine</u> 30:11-12, December 1950.

1283 Ebel, Otto. <u>Women Composers; A Biographical Handbook of Woman's Work in Music</u>. Brooklyn, N.Y.: F. H. Chandler, 1902.
   "Writers and works of musical literature have been included."--Preface.

1284 Edmunds, John, and Boelzner, Gordon. <u>Some Twentieth Century American Composers; A Selective Bibliography</u>. New York: New York Public Library, 1959.
   Significant material on one woman, Peggy Glanville-Hicks, is included in Volume 2, pp. 31-32. There are 45 bibliographical entries on writings about and by her.

1285 Feather, Leonard G. <u>The New Edition of the Encyclopedia of Jazz</u>. 2 vols. New York: Horizon Press, 1960.
   In addition to the biographical information included for jazz musicians, there are a number of photographs of the most prominent musicians. Among these are many women such as Bessie Smith, Billie Holiday, and Mahalia Jackson.

163 Bibliographies, Dictionaries

1286 Hall, Jacob Henry. Biography of Gospel Songs and Hymn Writers. New York: AMS Press, 1971, c1914.
Women are discussed in over 10 per cent of the biographies in this work. Composers of the early 1800's and early 1900's are included.

1287 Hixon, Donald L. Music in Early America: A Bibliography of Music in Evans. Metuchen, N.J.: Scarecrow Press, 1970.
A number of women's compositions are listed in Evans' American Bibliography and the Early American Imprints, 1639-1800.

1288 _____ and Hennessee, Don A. Women in Music: A Biobibliography. Metuchen, N.J.: Scarecrow Press, 1975.
Biographical material for over 4,000 women in music from all countries and all periods of music.

1289 Hughes, Rupert. American Composers; A Study of the Music of This Country and of Its Future, with Biographies of the Leading Composers of the Present Time. New York: AMS Press, 1973, c1914.
This is a revised edition of the earlier work Contemporary American Composers and contains additional chapters by Arthur Elson.

1290 Ireland, Norma Olin. Index to Women of the World from Ancient to Modern Times: Biographies and Portraits. Westwood, Mass.: F. W. Faxon Co., 1970.
A section emphasizes the relationship of women to music.

1291 Johnson, Harold Earle. Operas on American Subjects. New York: Coleman-Ross, 1964.
Many of the operas listed are written by Americans including women.

1292 Jones, F. O. A Handbook of American Music and Musicians, Containing Biographies of American Musicians and Histories of the Principal Musical Institutions, Firms, and Societies. New York: Da Capo Press, 1971, c1886.
This is arranged in dictionary form and includes many women.

1293 Lawless, Ray McKinley. Folksingers and Folksongs in America; A Handbook of Biography, Bibliography, and Discography. Rev. ed. New York: Duell, Sloan and Pearce, 1965.
   Information on many folksingers can be found in this work.

1294 Locke, Arthur Ware, and Fassett, Charles K. Selected List of Choruses for Women's Voices. 3rd ed. Northampton, Mass.: Smith College, 1964.
   An extensive list of works for treble or equal voices. Difficulty, voicing, duration, publishers, and source of text is given.

1295 Malone, Bill C., and McCulloh, Judith. Stars of Country Music; Uncle Dave Macon to Johnny Rodriguez. Urbana: University of Illinois Press, 1975.
   Biographies of U.S. country musicians. One chapter is devoted to Loretta Lynn, and one section is entitled "The 'New Breed' and the 'New Women.'"

1296 Musical America: Directory Issue. Great Barrington, Mass.: Billboard Publications, 1868/69-
   A directory of Americans which is updated regularly.

1297 Paid My Dues. Milwaukee, Woman's Soul Pub., 1974- .
   A quarterly journal of women and music that began publication in 1974.

1298 Pavlakis, Christopher. The American Music Handbook. New York: Free Press, 1974.
   A directory of American music.

1299 Reis, Claire Raphael. Composers in America: Biographical Sketches of Contemporary Composers with a Record of Their Works, 1912-1937. Rev. ed. New York: Macmillan, 1947.
   An extensive compilation of American composers through the first half of the twentieth century. Some of the women composers included are Louise Talma, Ruth Crawford Seeger, and Mary Howe.

1300 Saleski, Gdal. Famous Musicians of Jewish Origin. New York: Bloch Pub. Co., 1949.
   Bibliographies of these musicians are divided into sections by composers, conductors, violinists, etc.

165 Bibliographies, Dictionaries

A number of American women can be found, especially in the section on pianists and singers.

1301 Sonneck, Oscar George Theodore. Bibliography of Early Secular American Music. Washington, D.C.: H. L. McQueen, 1905.
Several women composers are included. The partially annotated index is helpful for locating information on women.

1302 Stambler, Irwin. Encyclopedia of Folk, Country and Western Music. New York: St. Martin's Press, 1969.
Biographical information is given for many musicians in folk, country and western music, including a number of women in these fields.

1303 _____. Encyclopedia of Pop, Rock and Soul. New York: St. Martin's Press, 1974.
A compilation of popular music history which includes many women in the popular music field.

1304 Ulanov, Barry. A Handbook of Jazz. New York: Viking Press, 1957.
This handbook consists of essays on various aspects of jazz. Appendix A, "The Musicians of Jazz," includes short biographies of Bessie Smith and Billie Holiday.

1305 Williams, Ora. American Black Women in the Arts and Social Sciences; A Bibliographic Survey. Metuchen, N.J.: Scarecrow Press, 1973.
This work is a valuable source for identifying black women composers plus their works and publishers. Ms. Williams concedes that the section on musicians was the most difficult part of her research. She has also listed books and articles by and/or about black women in music.

INDEX OF NAMES

Abel, Mrs. I. 329
Adams, John Clarke 330
Adams, Juliette Crosby 174
Adams, M. 48
Ahlers, Margaret Ann 49
Albee, Edward 624
Albertson, Chris 50, 51, 67, 96
Alboni, Marietta 26, 299
Albus, Harry James 332
Alda, Frances 52
Aldrich, Richard 53, 54
Alexander, Lucille Dillinger 333
Allen, Betty 652
Alterman, Loraine 334, 336
Altman, Thelma 337
Alvarez, Marguerite d' 55
Alverson, Rosana Margaret Blake 56
Ames, Morgan 57
Anderson, Ada Mae 835
Anderson, Ivie Mary 1003
Anderson, Lynn 539
Anderson, Marian 324, 332, 340, 341, 379, 383, 394, 395, 524, 528, 559, 647, 663, 678, 732, 757, 809, 876, 884, 929, 965, 1002, 1046, 1083, 1088, 1095, 1096, 1112, 1241, 1243, 1247, 1252

Anderton, Margaret 58, 59, 60
Andrews, Frances M. 1099
Andrews Sisters 429
Angelou, M. 342
Anka, Paul 548
Anthony, Doriot 414
Apel, Paul Hermann 344
Appleton, Jane Scovell 345
Ardoin, John 346, 347
Arell, Ruth 348, 349
Arian, Edward 63
Arlyck, Diana Miller 350
Arment, Hollace Elbert 351
Armsby, Leonora Wood 64, 352
Armstrong, Donald Jan 353
Armstrong, Lil Hardin <u>see</u> Hardin, Lil
Armstrong, William 65, 66
Aronowitz, Alfred G. 354, 355
Arstein, Helen 671
Ashley, Patricia 356
Asklund, Gunnar 357, 358
Atkinson, N. 360
Attwood, Martha 247
Avery, Paul 363
Ayars, Christine Merrick 1178

Baccaloni, Salvatore 985

Index of Names

Bachauer, Gina 498
Baer, B. 367
Baez, Joan 368, 408, 449, 488, 494, 529, 557, 573, 711, 827, 828, 1007
Bailey, Mildred 377
Bailey, Pearl 369, 370
Baily, Evangeline 1021
Baird, Pat 371
Baker, David 372
Baker, Martha Atwood 85
Bakke, Josephine 112
Baldwin, Lillian 206
Ballard, Florence 558, 829, 1059
Ballard, P. 373
Balliett, Whitney 67, 374, 375, 376, 377
Baral, Robert 69
Barclay, Nicoel 890
Barnes, Edwin Ninyon Chaloner 1179, 1180
Barnes, Nancy 378
Barnum, P. T. 40, 45, 54
Barrell, Edgar A. 70
Barrett, Emma 767, 1240
Barrientos, M. 71
Bart, Teddy 380
Barzun, Jacques 381
Bates, Blanche 761
Bauer, E. F. 72
Bauer, Marion 1178, 1181, 1221
Baxter, Clairce Howard 1273
Beach, Mrs. H. H. A. (Amy Marcy Cheney) 73, 76, 166, 245, 270, 317, 344, 356, 418, 1178, 1181, 1221, 1222
Bean, Helen J. 1182
Beatles 943
Becker, Paula 384
Beckley, Paul V. 385
Behrens, E. 386
Bell Sisters 391

Bellows, George Kent 1221
Belz, Carl 387
Bender, W. 388, 389
Benét, Laura 14
Bergman, Nancy 390
Bernard, S. 392
Bernstein, Ellen 797
Bernstein, Leonard 331
Biancolli, Louis 130
Bickford, Vahdah Olcott 872
Big Brother and the Holding Company 786, 914
Bims, Hamilton 394
Bing, Rudolf 395, 412
Birge, Edward Bailey 1183
Birnie, W. A. 396
Blesh, Rudi 75
Bley, Carla 694, 1127
Block, Adrienne Fried 397, 398
Bloom, Clifford 76
Bloomfield, Arthur J. 399
Bluebelles 693
Blum, Daniel C. 1184
Boeckman, Charles 402
Boelzner, Gordon 1284
Bond, Margaret 929
Bond, V. 404
Bono, Cher see Cher
Bordoni, Faustina 22
Borroff, Edith 1185
Boulanger, Lilli 314
Boulanger, Nadia 331, 347, 466, 486, 733, 984, 1044, 1081, 1082
Bowen, C. D. 406
Bowen, Jean 407
Brackett, Anna Callender 77
Brainard, Kate J. 315
Brand, Oscar 408
Branscombe, G. 409
Brant, LeRoy V. 410
Brico, Antonia 61, 62, 124, 246, 319, 491, 814, 950

Index of Names

Briggs, John 412, 413
Briggs, Marion L. 414
Britain, Radie 1186
Brockway, Wallace 1187
Brook, Donald 416
Brooker, Beryl 534
Brooks, Benjamin 418
Brooks, Jessie Mae 835
Brower, Edith 78
Brower, Harriette 79, 80, 81
Brown, Geoff 419
Brown, Les 1015
Brown, Lillyn 738
Brown, Nellie E. 297
Brown, Mrs. P. H. 82
Brown, Toni 890
Bryant, Anita 420, 421
Bryant, Celia Mae 1099
Bryant, Felice 912
Bucci, Jerry Michael 422
Buehlman, Barbara 423
Bulman, Joan 15
Bundy, June 424, 425
Burns, Don 1188
Burnsworth, Charles Carl 1275
Burr, H. H. 83
Burton, Jack 1189, 1190
Butler, Blanche 426
Butterfield, H. M. 427

Cage, Ruth 428
Cahoon, Helen Fouts 429
Caldwell, Sarah 345, 389, 500, 504, 550, 631, 654, 690, 740, 861, 915, 962, 1010, 1090
Callas, Evangelia 430
Callas, Maria Meneghini 330, 346, 412, 413, 430, 431, 440, 441, 448, 475, 554, 576, 697, 707, 729, 757, 892, 928, 947, 995, 1057, 1126, 1151

Calton, David 432
Calvé, Emma 305, 323
Calvin, S. 433
Cantwell, Jean Baker 434
Caracappa, Michael 435
Cardus, Neville 436
Carlton, Jean 975
Carmichael, Carol 438
Carreño, Teresa 216
Carroll, Barbara 533, 535
Carroll, Diahann 415, 520, 526, 716, 899, 1068
Carson, Norma 537
Carter, Maybelle 816
Casale, Giac 440
Case, Anna 279
Cavanah, Frances 16
Celli, Teodoro 441
Chandler, Dorothy 734
Charters, Samuel Barclay 86, 87, 88, 1191
Chase, Gilbert 1192
Cheney, Amy Marcy see Beach, Mrs. H. H. A.
Cher 687
Chilton, John 443
Chotzinoff, Samuel 444
Christgau, Georgia 445, 446
Claghorn, Charles Eugene 1276
Clark, N. M. 89
Clark, Petula 608, 637
Clark, Robert S. 448
Clarke, Rebecca 36
Clayton, Ellen Creathorne 1
Clugoszewski, Lucia 1081
Cohen, John 449
Colbert, Warren E. 1277
Cole, Mrs. Nat King 450
Coleman, Emily 451, 452, 453
Coleman, Henry 454
Collier, Graham 455
Collins, ElVera 456

Collins, Judy 457, 557
Collis, J. 458
Colson, Percy 90
Comfort, Annabel 91
Commanday, Robert 460, 461
Cone, John Frederick 92
Connor, Anthony 868
Contos, Catherine 462
Cook, Bruce 1193
Cook, Faith Reyher 464
Cook, Ida 1194
Cooke, James Francis 94-95
Coolidge, Elizabeth 72, 675
Coolidge, Rita 722, 890
Coon, Caroline 465
Cooper, Arthur 96
Copland, Aaron 331, 466, 486, 733, 1082
Coppage, Noel 467, 468
Corbin, John 97
Cornell, Helen Loftin 469
Cornish, Nellie Centennial 470
Cotton, John 2
Cox, Marian 199
Craig, M. 472
Creed, Linda 912
Crichton, Kyle Samuel 473
Crider, E. O. 474
Cron, Theodore O. 1195
Cross, D. 475
Cuff, J. 476
Cugat, Lorraine (Mrs. Xavier) 667, 668
Cushing, Mary Finch Watkins 98, 99, 100, 477

Dachs, David 478
Dale, Clamma 411, 447
Dallas, K. 479, 480
Dalton, David 481
Dalton, M. A. 482
Dance, Stanley 101
Dane, Barbara 609, 635

Daniels, M. 1196
Daniels, Mabel 831
D'Aranyi, Adila 194
D'Aranyi, Hortense Emilia 194
D'Aranyi, Jelly 194
Daughtry, Willia Estelle 102
Davidson, Gladys 1278, 1279
Davis, Jean 1169
Davis, M. 103
Davis, Ronald L. 1197
Dawbarn, B. 483
Day, Doris 1015, 1975
Deadly Nightshade 819
Dean, F. 104
De Bidoli, Emi 484
Debrant, Cyr 105
De Guichard, Ann 405
Deiro, Pietro 456
De Koven, Anna Farwell 106
De LaGrange, Henry-Louis 486
De Lorenzo, Leonard 487
Denisoff, R. Serge 488
Dennis, Charles M. 489
De Pauw, Linda Grant 3
Derhen, Andrew 490, 491
De Schauensee, Max 492
Dessoff, Margarete 80
De Toledano, Ralph 493
Detzer, K. 495
De Turk, David A. 494
Diemer, Emma Lou 730
Dlugoszewski, Lucia 699
Dobson, Bonnie 557
Dotson, Sally 893
Douglass, Fannie Howard 663
Drinker, Harry 359
Drinker, Sophie Lewis 359, 501, 618, 1199, 1281, 1282
Drummond, Robert Rutherford 107
Dufty, William 665

Duke, Laura 236
Dunlap, Agnes Mary Robertson 17
Duston, A. 502
Dutton, William S. 503
Dyer, R. 504
Dylan, Bob 529
Dyler, W. 505

Eames, Emma 305
Easton, Florence 238
Eaton, Quaintance 108, 109, 506, 507, 1200, 1201
Ebel, Otto 1283
Eberhart, Jonathan 508
Eckstein, Elsie 381
Edmunds, John 1284
Edwards, E. Harlow 110
Edwards, J. S. 509
Eldred, Patricia Mulrooney 511
Ellington, Edward Kennedy (Duke) 515, 899
Ellingwood, Leonard 1202
Elliot, Cass 605, 728, 841, 889, 918
Ellis, Anita 376
Elson, Arthur 1203, 1289
Elson, James 516
Elson, Louis Charles 1204, 1205
Engel, Carl 1206
Engel, Lehman 1207
English, M. 517
English, Mary E. 518
Epstein, Edward Z. 844
Epstein, M. 521
Erb, J. Lawrence 111
Erhardt-Snyder, William 522
Escot, Pozzi 729
Everly Brothers 548
Ewen, David 524, 1208, 1209, 1210, 1211, 1212

Fanny 371, 527, 542, 987, 1043
Fariña, Richard 529
Farnsworth, Paul R. 530
Farrar, Geraldine 97, 113, 114, 115, 177, 203, 306, 312, 492
Farrell, Eileen 973, 1057
Fassett, Charles K. 1294
Faull, Ellen 946
Favis-Artsay, A. 531
Feather, Leonard 533, 534, 535, 536, 537, 1213, 1285
Fellows, Myles 538
Fenwick, George Roy 1214
Ferguson, Charles W. 546
Ferrier, Kathleen 436, 547
Ferrier, Winifred 547
Ferris, George Titus 22
Ffrench, Florence 116
Finck, Henry Theophilus 117, 118, 119
Fine, Vivian 969, 1081
Finn, William J. 549
Fischer, D. B. 120
Fishel, Elizabeth 552
Fisher, Renee B. 553
Fisher, Mrs. William Arms 60
Fitzgerald, Ella 88, 493, 512, 513, 514, 515, 523, 553, 934, 996, 1134, 1140, 1149
Fitzgerald, Gerald 346, 554, 555
Fitzlyon, April 556
Flack, Roberta 567, 581, 689, 746, 840, 848, 1130
Flagstad, Kirsten 292
Fleming, Rhonda 561
Fleming, Virginia 946
Fletcher, Tom 121
Foote, Margaret 563

Ford, F. G. 122
Forsee, Aylesa 559
Forster, P. 560
Foster, O. H. 123
Fowler, Charles B. 562
Frame, Florence K. 124, 563
Frank, Gerold 564
Franklin, Aretha 367, 553, 573, 582, 656, 702, 735, 745, 750, 787, 793, 827, 972, 991, 1064, 1093, 1100, 1255
Franklin, C. J. 125
Frederick, R. 566
Freedland, Nat 567, 568
Freeman, John W. 569
Freer, E. E. 126
Fremstad, Olive 100
Fretwell, Dorrie S. 570
Friedman, Myra 571
Fudger, M. 572
Fuller Sisters 128

Gadski, Madame 226
Gahr, David 573
Galli-Curci, Amelita 188, 203
Garcia, Maria 256
Garcia, Pauline 256
Garden, Mary 92, 108, 129, 211, 385, 538, 545, 813, 1116
Gardner, Julie 1169
Gardner, Mark 579
Garland, Judy 564, 844, 1092, 1251
Garland, Phyl 580, 581, 582
Garthwaite, Terry 446
Gatti-Casazza, Guilo 131, 132, 309
Gaul, H. B. 133
Gaume, Mary Matilda 134
Gehrkens, Karl W. 583, 584

Gelatt, Roland 585, 586
Gentry, Bobbie 401, 1035
Gerber, Aimé 153
Gerhardt, Elena 587
Gerke, Madge Cathcart 588
Gerow, Maurice 1070
Gibson, Barbara 662
Gideon, Miriam 525, 831, 905, 968, 969, 1217
Gilhagen, E. 135, 136
Gilman, Lawrence 137
Gipson, Richard M. 138
Gishford, Anthony 1216
Glackens, Ira 139
Glanville-Hicks, Peggy 344, 362, 1081, 1082, 1284
Glenn, C. 599
Goldberg, Isaac 140
Goldblatt, Burt 1195
Golden, Lotti 593
Goldflower 542
Goldman, Albert 601, 602, 603
Goldreich, Ester 604
Goldreich, Gloria 604
Goldstein, R. 605
Goldstein, Toby 606
Golton, G. R. 1153
Goreau, Laurraine 607
Gould, Glenn 608
Grafman, Howard 609
Graham, Billy 1125
Graham, Martha 945
Grau, R. 141
Graves, A. J. 24
Gravina, Peter 611
Gray, Doriana 404
Gray, Michael 612, 613, 614
Gray, N. J. 615
Grayson, Kathryn 358
Green, Benny 616
Green, M. S. 617
Green, Miriam 1217
Green, Stanley 1218

Index of Names

Greenbie, S. 618
Greene, Richard L. 619
Greenfield, Edward 620
Greenfield, Elizabeth Taylor 297
Grevatt, R. 621, 622, 623
Griffin, Bessie 649
Grimes, Sally 624
Groia, Philip 625
Groom, Bob 626
Grunfeld, Frederic V. 627
Guertin, Paige 897

Hackett, K. 142
Hadden, J. Cuthbert 143, 144
Hadlock, Richard 145
Hageman, Richard 146
Haines, Connie 629
Haley, Alex 630
Hall, Jacob Henry 1286
Hall, Vera 778, 779
Hallock, M. 147
Hamblin, Dora Jane 631
Hamilton, J. 632
Hammerstein, Oscar 92, 148
Hammond, J. 633
Handly, Donna 356, 634
Hansen, Barry 635
Hardin, Lil 225, 250, 1102, 1141
Hare, Maud Cuney 149
Harman, Carter 637
Harris, Kenn 638
Harris, Margaret 639
Harris, Roy 486
Harrison, Mildred 363
Hart, Hattie 236, 867
Hartt, R. L. 150
Harwood, R. P. 641
Hauk, Minnie 5, 109, 151, 197, 295, 1238
Havener, H. 642
Hawes, Bess 664
Hawkins, M. 643

Hawkins, Mrs. Robert 644, 645
Hayes, C. J. 646
Hayes, Catherine 299
Hayes, Roland 650
Hays, William 647
Hebson, Ann 648
Heilbut, Tony 649
Helm, MacKinley 650
Helman, H. 651
Hemming, Roy 652, 653
Henahan, D. 654
Henderson, Jerry 1071
Henderson, Rosa 739
Henderson, William James 655
Hendrix, Jimi 388, 706
Hennessee, Don A. 1288
Henninges, Dora 315
Henshaw, L. 656
Hentoff, Nat 657, 658, 659, 988, 989
Hess, Myra 585
Hester, Juliette 557
Hetherington, John 152
Heylbut, Rose 153, 660, 661, 662
Hickerson, Patricia 674
Hill, Dorothy 417
Hill, Golden 577
Hill, Roy 663
Hillis, Margaret 799
Hipsher, Edward Ellsworth 154, 155
Hitchcock, Hugh Wiley 1219
Hixon, Donald L. 1287, 1288
Hodges, Betty 895
Holiday, Billie 374, 377, 443, 523, 536, 553, 602, 616, 659, 665, 702, 703, 947, 977, 989, 1070, 1072, 1102, 1139, 1142, 1143, 1144, 1149, 1251, 1285, 1304
Holloway, Nancy 865

Index of Names 174

Holly, Hal 666, 667, 668
Homer, L. 159
Hope, Lynn 953
Hopkins, Jerome 160
Horne, Lena 515, 640,
 670, 671, 672, 762,
 817, 824
Horne, Marilyn 973
Hourigan, Virginia 673
Howard, George S. 674
Howard, John Tasker 162,
 1220, 1221
Howard, Kathleen 163
Howe, Mark Anthony De
 Wolfe 675
Howe, Mary 525, 1221,
 1299
Hubbard, William Lines
 1222
Hughes, Adella Prentiss 202
Hughes, Allen 676
Hughes, E. 164
Hughes, Rupert 165, 166,
 1289
Humes, Helen 376
Humphrey, Laning 26
Huneker, J. G. 167, 168
Hunt, Conover 3
Hunt, M. 677
Hurok, S. 678
Hutchins, Carleen Maley
 508
Hyers, Anna 297
Hyers, Emma 297

Ike & Tina Turner 680
Ingram, M. D. 681
Ireland, Norma Olin 1290
Irons, M. E. 169
Irving, Clive 682
Irwin, May 75

Jackson, George Stuyvesant
 27
Jackson, Jesse 685
Jackson, Mahalia 375, 376,
 607, 609, 630, 646,
 647, 649, 685, 686,
 702, 708, 794, 795,
 801, 802, 803, 854,
 855, 863, 941, 1014,
 1020, 1069, 1085, 1087,
 1173, 1285
Jacobs, Linda 687, 688,
 689
Jacobs-Bond, Carrie 89
Jacobson, R. 690, 691
Janis, Byron 964
Janis, Harriet 75
Jasper, Tony 692
Jefferson, Margo 693,
 694, 695, 696
Jefferson Airplane 605,
 1145
Jellinek, George 697
Jeritza, Maria 171, 172,
 203, 238
Joe, R. 698
Johnson, Frances Hall
 173
Johnson, Harold Earle
 4, 1223, 1291
Johnson, Helen 1224
Johnson, Leonore 674
Johnson, Tom 699, 700
Johnson, W. D. 701
Jones, Elayne 460
Jones, F. O. 1292
Jones, Hettie 702
Jones, LeRoi 703
Jones, R. P. 704
Jones, Sissieretta 102,
 196, 265
Joplin, Janis 388, 400,
 432, 481, 571, 572, 578,
 601, 605, 706, 749, 750,
 786, 827, 866, 902, 914,
 918, 991, 1026, 1193
Jorgensen, J. 705
Josephson, M. 706
Joslyn, Jay 707
Joy of Cooking 446, 542
Jubilee Singers 201

Index of Names

Kahn, D. 709
Kahn, Kath 710
Kalish, E. 711
Kefalas, Elinor 714
Keller, Helen 661
Keller, V. B. 715
Kelley, Mrs. Edgar Stillman 175
Kellogg, Clara Louise 109, 176, 197, 295
Kelly, V. 716
Kemp, Dorothy E. 717
Kempf, Paul 177
Kennedy, J. B. 178
Kennedy, P. 718
Kennely, P. 719
Kettring, Donald D. 720
King, Carole 392, 468, 722, 750, 830, 1093
Kinne, Margaret 723
Kirby, F. 724
Kirsten, Dorothy 725
Kloman, William 728
Kmen, Henry 5
Knight, Janet 729
Knight, Marie 705
Knowles, Alison 700
Kobbé, Gustav 179
Kolb, Barbara 343
Kolodin, Irving 731, 732, 733, 1225
Koopal, Grace G. 734
Korall, G. 735
Korn, Clara A. 166
Krebs, T. L. 180
Krehm, Ida 736
Kubly, Herbert 1226
Kuflik, A. 963
Kunkel, Marjorie 737
Kunstadt, L. 738, 739
Kupferberg, Herbert 740, 741

LaBelle, Patti 693
Ladd, George Trumbull 181
La Farge, Peter 747

Lage, Wally 748
Lahee, Henry Charles 182, 1227, 1228, 1229
Landau, Deborah 749
Landau, Jon 750
Landis, Ellen 720
Landis, Kenneth L. 720
Landon, Grelun 1035
Landver, Rose 1045
Lang, Paul Henry 1230
Lang, Margaret Ruthven 166
Larkin, Margaret 183
Larkin, Philip 751
Larsen, Arved M. 752
Laufe, Abe 1231
Laufer, Beatrice 753
Laurie, J. 754
Lawless, Ray McKinley 1293
Lawrence, Marjorie 91, 660, 755
Lawrence, Robert 756, 757
Lawrence, Vera Brodsky 6
Lawton, Mary 184
Lee, Bertha 86
Lee, Brenda 992
Lee, Janet A. 759
Lee, Peggy 653, 1075, 1140, 1251
Lees, Gene 760
Leff, L. J. 761
Leginska, Ethel 313, 319
Lehmann, Lilli 185, 260, 305
Lehmann, Lotte 186, 187, 524, 1253, 1264
Leigh, Carolyn 439
Le Massena, Clarence Edward 188
Leonard, Eugenie Andruss 7
Leonard, Florence 189
Leonard, Neil 763
Lerman, Leo 766, 767, 768, 769

Index of Names

Levi, Jeannette 979
Levi, Nanette 474
Levison, E. 771
Levy, Lester 29, 30
Liesen, Philomene 772
Lind, Jenny 13, 14, 15,
    16, 17, 18, 20, 22,
    26, 32, 40, 41, 44,
    45, 54, 256, 299,
    1116, 1234, 1238,
    1248, 1252
Little, Lowell 776
Livermore, Mary A. 315
Livingstone, W. 777
Lloyd, Alice 754
Lockard, Thaddeus C. 45
Locke, Arthur Ware 1294
Loesser, Arthur 1232
Lomas, Alan 1233
Lomax, Alan 778, 779
London, George 780
Lonergan, Elizabeth 190
Longstreet, Stephen 781
Lorillard, Elaine 510
Lowry, A. 783
Lucas, B. 785
Luc-Gabrielle, Sister 784
Lydon, Michael 786, 787
Lynn, Judy 1159
Lynn, Loretta 467, 788,
    1035, 1295
Lyon, Hugh Lee 789

McCall, A. B. 191
McCarrell, Lamar K. 790
McCormack, Lily Foley 192
McCracken, James 791
McCulloh, Judith 1295
McCutcheon, Lynn Ellis
    792, 793
McDaniel, C. G. 794
McDearmon, Kay 795
McDonald, E. 796
McDonough, Jack 797,
    798
MacDowell, Edward 105

MacDowell, Mrs. Edward
    193, 261
McElroy, George 799
MacGregor, Evelyn 1128
MacInnes, Idamay 476
Mackin, Tom 800
Macleod, Joseph 194
McRae, B. 195
Madeira, Louis Cephas
    1234
Maier, Guy 804, 805
Mainwaring, Fredrica 806
Majors, M. A. 196
Malibran, Maria Felicia
    1041, 1237
Malone, Bill C. 1295
Mamas and the Papas 605,
    692, 728, 841
Mander, Raymond 1235
Manning, B. T. 609
Mapleson, James Henry
    197
Marcus, Adele 964
Marcus, Greil 808
Marcuse, Maxwell F.
    1236
Marek, George Richard
    1237
Maretzek, Max 31, 198
Marks, Edward Bennet
    200, 1238
Marsh, D. 810
Marsh, J. B. T. 201
Marsh, Robert Charles 202
Martens, Frederick Herman 203
Martin, Deac C. T. 1239
Martin, Mary 429, 812,
    877, 1231
Martin, Sallie 649
Martin, Sara 958
Martinez, Raymond Joseph
    1240
Marx, H. 813
Mason, Daniel Gregory
    204
Mates, Julian 8

Matthews, Thomas 1241
Matz, Mary Jane 815, 1242, 1243
Maude, Mrs. Raymond 32
Maxwell, Elsa 286
May, E. C. 205
Maynard, Clarke 206
Maynor, Dorothy 546
Mayor, Martin 817, 818
Melanson, J. 819
Melba, Nellie 90, 152, 207, 208, 209, 221, 304, 305, 310
Mellers, Wilfrid Howard 1244
Mellish, Mary Flannery 210
Meltz, Ramona J. 674, 820
Meltzer, C. H. 211
Merington, M. 213
Merker, E. 821
Merkling, Frank 822, 1245
Merman, Ethel 823, 1231, 1251
Merritt, Kathleen 713
Meryman, R. 824
Merz, Karl 214
Meyer, Annie 215
Meyer, Hazel 826
Micklo, Ann Marie 827
Midler, Bette 683, 887
Milan, Judith 828
Milanov, Zinka 1126
Milinowski, Marta 216
Millay, Edna St. Vincent 1271
Miller, E. 829, 830
Miller, M. 217
Miller, Philip L. 831
Mills, Stephanie 858, 878
Minelli, Liza 887
Minson, M. B. 834
Mitchell, George 835
Mitchell, Joni 468, 573, 593, 750, 769, 937, 976
Mitchenson, Joe 1235
Moffo, Anna 796, 895
Moncrieff, Gladys 836
Moneak, Elena 58
Monson, Karen 837
Montagu, Ashley 838
Monteith, Ann K. 839
Moore, Eleanor 840
Moore, Frank 33
Moore, Gerald 841
Moore, Grace 219, 524, 985
Moore, June 842
Moore, Mary Carr 155
Moore, Undine 929
Moppets 846
More, D. 220
Morella, Joe 844
Morgan, Alfred Lindsay 845
Morschauser, J. 846
Morse, Charles 847, 878
Morse, David 849
Moss, Carlton 671
Mothersingers 169, 489
Mothner, Ira 853
Moulton, Mrs. Charles 34
Mozart, Nannerl 1028
Mueller, John Henry 856
Murphy, Agnes G. 221
Murphy, R. 857
Murtagh, Rena 1246
Musser, Willard I. 862
Mussulman, Joseph A. 224
Myrus, Donald 863

Nanry, Charles 866
Napier, Simon A. 867
Near, Holly 552
Nearing, Nellis M. S. 226
Nearing, Scott 226
Neff, Robert 868
Nelson, J. 869
Nelson, Mary Jarman 870

Index of Names

Nettl, Paul 871
Nevin, Ethelbert 105
Newman, Mrs. M. W. 875
Newman, Shirlee Petkin 876, 877
Newton-John, Olivia 467, 688
Ney, Elly 189
Nikolaieff, George 878
Nilsson, Birgit 731, 973, 1057
Nitty Gritty Dirt Band 1176
Noble, Helen Klaffky 879
Norcott, B. J. 880
Nordica, Lillian 108, 139, 227, 228, 295, 304, 305, 327, 1249
Northcutt, John Orlando 229, 881
Novaes, Guiomar 498
Novak, B. J. 883
Nugent, Maude 140, 1190
Nyro, Laura 976

Oliver, Marie 886
Oliver, Paul 230, 231, 232, 233, 234
Oliveros, Pauline 714, 1217
Olsson, Bengt 236
Ono, Yoko 679
Oppenheimer, Peer J. 889
Orloff, Katherine 890
Orth, Maureen 891
Osborne, Conrad L. 892
Oster, Harry 893
Ostransky, Leroy 894

Page, Patti 992
Pahlen, Kurt 1247
Paige, Raymond 896
Panassié, Hughes 240, 898
Panser, R. M. 241
Parker, D. C. 170, 900

Parker, Henry Taylor 242
Partridge, Robert 901
Pastor, Tony 200
Patten, M. 243
Patti, Adelina 13, 22, 26, 54, 330, 1237, 1238
Patton, Charley 86
Patton, James Welch 42
Paul, Doris A. 903
Paul, Elliot 1248
Pavlakis, Christopher 1298
Pearl, Minnie 833
Peltz, Mary Ellis Opdycke 244, 1249, 1250
Perle, George 905
Pert, Yvonne 245
Peter, Paul & Mary 355, 853
Peters, A. 906
Peters, Roberta 907, 1243
Petrides, Frederique 246
Peyser, Ethel R. 247, 1181
Pfautsch, Lloyd 908
Philips, Mary 909
Phillips, Burrill 831
Phillips, Ester 868
Phillips, Karen 910
Phillips, Michelle 728, 841
Pichierri, Louis 9
Pierce, Billie 893
Playmates 548
Pleasants, Henry 1251, 1252
Podis, Eunice 911
Pointer Sisters 891, 1019, 1148
Polk, Videt 1273
Pollock, Bruce 912
Pons, Lily 464, 524, 598, 1055, 1062
Ponselle, Rosa 154, 238
Ponzo, Marie 913
Poppy, John 914
Porter, Andrew 915

Poulin, A. 494
Powell, Mary 1226
Preston, Stuart 1253
Previn, Dory 1027
Price, Leontyne 394, 399,
 413, 440, 444, 452, 555,
 764, 765, 789, 825, 857,
 904, 917, 929, 965, 973,
 974, 997, 1040, 1057,
 1089, 1115, 1197, 1241,
 1247
Pride of Women 542
Putnam, A. 248

Ragan, Elnor S. 919
Rainey, Gertrude "Ma"
 195, 225, 232, 233,
 272, 282, 702, 863,
 1048, 1070, 1141
Ramsey, Frederic 250
Ran, Shulamit 837
Ray, Carline 1169
Reddy, Helen 567, 939,
 1093
Redfield, Liza 730, 770
Reed, Carol 540
Reed, R. 920
Reeves, Martha 811, 849
Reiner, Mildred 674
Reinhart, Carole Dawn
 999
Reis, Clair Raphael 251,
 252, 1299
Revelli, William D. 922
Reynolds, Malvina 760
Riale, Karen 712
Ricapito, Joseph A. 923
Richter, M. M. 924
Riddle, Almeda 925
Riperton, Minnie 696, 785
Ritchie, Jean 408, 609,
 926, 1036, 1133
Rittenhouse, Carl H. 927
Ritter, Mrs. Frances
 Malone 37, 253
Ritter, Frederic Louis
 1254

Rizzo, Francis 928
Roach, Hildred 929
Roberti, Margherita 895
Roberts, Joan 930
Roberts, John S. 931
Robinson, Francis 932
Robinson, Louie 933, 934,
 935, 936
Rodnitzky, Jerome L. 939
Roesch, C. B. 940
Rogers, C. 941
Rogers, Clara Kathleen
 254, 255
Rogers, F. 10
Rogers, Francis 256
Romaguoll, M. 942
Ronettes 943
Ronstadt, Linda 722
Rorem, Ned 944, 945,
 946, 947, 948
Rosen, Judith 949
Rosen, Marjorie 950
Rosenthal, Harold D. 951,
 952
Ross, Diana 366, 511,
 829, 936, 1059
Ross, Kate 75
Rotante, A. 953
Roth, Henry 954
Roussel, Hubert 955
Rubin-Rabson, Grace 949
Rublowsky, John 1255,
 1256
Rush, [Dr.] 38
Rushmore, Robert 957
Russell, Frank 39
Russell, Jane 561
Russell, Tony 958
Rutledge, Virginia 1159
Ryder, G. A. 959

Saal, Hubert 960, 961,
 962, 963
Sabin, Robert 964, 965
Sablosky, Irving L. 1257
Sachse, Julius Fredrich
 257

Index of Names

Safka, Melanie 912
Sainte-Marie, Buffy 747, 912
Saks, Toby 966
Saleski, Gdal 1300
Samaroff Stokowski, Olga 258
Saminsky, Lazare 969
Samuels, Charles 1124
Sander, Ellen 970, 971
Sanders, Charles L. 972
Sargeant, Winthrop 259, 973, 974, 975
Sarlin, Bob 976
Saxon, Michele 966
Schaun, George 1258
Scherman, Bernardine Kielty 40
Schickel, Richard 672, 1259
Schiffman, Jack 977
Schmidt, Arthur P. 287
Schneir, Miriam 3
Schoen-René, Anna Eugénie 260
Scholes, Percy Alfred 261
Schonberg, Harold C. 978
Schuller, Gunther 262
Schumann-Heink, E. 184, 263, 264
Scott, Mrs. Carlyle 1261
Scott, Hazel 695
Scruggs, Lawson Andrew 265
Seagle, Helen 979
Seeger, Peter 980
Seeger, Ruth Crawford 136, 362, 729, 962, 968, 1299
Seligman, Paul 981
Selner, J. C. 982
Seltsam, William H. 266
Seltzer, George 983
Sembrich, M. 267
Sembrich, Marcella 127, 305
Sessions, Roger 331

Shanet, Howard 1260
Shapiro, Eudice 954
Shapiro, Lynne D. 987
Shapiro, Nat 988, 989
Shapiro, S. 990
Shaw, Allen 867
Shaw, Arnold 991, 992, 993, 994
Shawe-Taylor, D. 995
Sheean, Vincent 997
Shelton, Robert 573, 998
Shepherd, Jack 999
Sheppard, Sarah Hannah 325
Sherman, John K. 1000, 1261
Sherman, R. 1001
Shirley, George 1002
Short, Bobby 1003
Shultz, Gladys Denny 41
Shumsky, Ellen 1006
Siegel, Al 396
Silberman, M. 1010
Sills, Beverly 556, 818, 973, 1011, 1040
Silverman, Jerry 1012
Simkins, Francis Butler 42
Simmonds, Bonnie 798
Simon, Carly 437, 567, 722, 847, 1013
Simon, G. 1014
Simon, George Thomas 1015, 1016
Simone, Nina 342, 580, 582, 602, 843, 1149
Simpson, Harold 1017
Slater, Jack 1019
Slick, Grace 468, 578, 605, 890, 918, 1145
Slonimsky, Nicolas 270, 1262
Smith, Bessie 50, 51, 57, 67, 74, 87, 88, 96, 101, 145, 195, 218, 225, 230, 231, 234, 235, 250, 259, 262,

Index of Names

272, 280, 282, 523, 605,
624, 647, 659, 702, 704,
749, 763, 826, 863, 894,
931, 988, 989, 1048,
1070, 1072, 1102, 1139,
1141, 1144, 1193, 1213,
1236, 1244, 1248, 1251,
1285, 1304
Smith, Bessie Mae (St. Louis Bessie) 234
Smith, Caroline Estes 271
Smith, Catherine Parons 1022
Smith, Cecil Michener 1263, 1264, 1265
Smith, Charles Edward 250, 272
Smith, Clara 958
Smith, E. R. 1023
Smith, Frances M. 273
Smith, Julia 831
Smith, Kate 1024
Smith, Mamie 1023, 1047
Smyth, Ethel Mary 274, 275, 320
Snyder, L. 276
Solomon, Izler 845
Somma, Robert 1026
Somogi, Judith 814
Sonneck, Oscar George Theodore 11, 12, 1301
Sontag, Henrietta 22, 39, 256, 299, 1234
Sorel, Claudette 1028, 1029
Sorrels, Rosalie 1030
Spaeth, Sigmund Gottfried 278, 1031, 1266
Speaks, C. P. 1032
Speer Family 384
Sperry, Gale L. 1033
Spiegel, B. 1034
Spitalny, Evelyn (Mrs. Phil) 1129
Spitalny, Phil 1015, 1129
Staffard, Jo 1005
Stambler, Irwin 1035

Stanley, M. 279
Starkie, Walter 1036
Starr, Susan 1037
Steane, J. B. 1040
Stearns, Marshall Winslow 280
Stedman, Jane W. 799, 1267
Stern, K. 1041
Sterrett, N. 1042
Sterritt, David 1043
Stevens, E. M. 1044
Stevens, Risë 473, 598, 979, 985, 1055
Stevenson, Florence 1045
Stevenson, Janet 1046
Stevenson, Robert Murrell 281
Stewart-Baxter, Derrick 282, 1047, 1048
Stickney, Doris 1049
Stoddard, Hope 1050, 1051, 1052, 1053
Stokowski, Leopold 321, 741
Storer, H. J. 283
Stoutamire, Albert 13
Strange, Lewis Clinton 284, 285
Stravinsky, Catherine 1054
Stravinsky, Igor 1054
Stravinsky, Theodore 1054
Strickland, Lilly 76
Strother, Cynthia 391
Strother, Kay 391
Stueckgold, Grete 99
Sundstrom, Ebba 289, 322
Supremes 366, 558, 594, 632, 692, 793, 829, 849, 1058, 1059
Surge, Frank 1060
Sutherland, Joan 620, 824, 973, 1057, 1061
Sutro, Florence Edith Clinton 288
Sutton, Horace 1062
Swan, Howard 1268

Index of Names

Swartout, Gladys 985
Sweet Adelines 390
Swinburne, J. 170
Swinyard, L. 1065
Syford, E. 290

Tallmadge, William H. 1069
Talma, Louise 525, 565, 831, 962, 968, 1081, 1082, 1299
Tanner, Paul 1070
Tassin, Myron 1071
Taubman, Hyman Howard 291
Taylor, Kay 1176
Taylor, L. M. 292
Taylor, Rae 1176
Tebaldi, Renata 638, 1057, 1126
Terkel, Studs 1072
Terrell, Tammi 906
Tetrazzini, Luiza 293
Teyte, Maggie 1073
Tharpe, Rosetta 977
Thebom, Blanche 410
Thillon, Anna 299
Thomas, Blanche 1240
Thomas, C. W. 1076
Thomas, D. 294, 1077
Thomas, Jean 294
Thomas, Tony 1078
Thomas Family 641
Thompson, Helen Mulford 1079
Thompson, Oscar 295
Thompson, Thomas 1080
Thomson, Virgil 331, 486, 1081, 1082, 1083
Thursby, Emma 138
Tick, Judith 296, 1084
Tiegel, E. 1085
Tobias, Tobi 1088
Todd, Arthur 1089
Tormé, Mel 1092
Trachter, Ira 1093
Tracy, Jack 537

Traubel, Helen 1017, 1094, 1249
Travers, Mary 355, 853
Trotter, James M. 297
Truette, Everette E. 1203
Truman, Margaret 1095, 1096
Tucker, B. 1097
Tucker, Tanya 1159
Turner, C. 298
Turner, Tina 680, 1086

Uggams, Leslie 920
Ulanov, Barry 1102, 1103, 1304
Ulehla, Ludmila 1217
Ulrich, Homer 1104
Underwood, John Levi 43
Upton, George Putnam 299, 300
Urmy, C. 301
Uselton, R. A. 1107

Valentry, Duane 1108
Vallée, Rudy 200
Vance, Marica 1111
Vandellas 811, 849
Van de Vate, Nancy 1109, 1110
Vaughan, Sarah 535, 579, 933, 992, 1080
Vehanen, Kosti 1112
Verrill, A. 1113
Viardot-García, Pauline 556
Votipka, Thelma 531

Wack, Harry Wellington 303
Wagenknecht, Edward Charles 44, 304, 1116
Wagnalls, Mabel 305, 306
Wagner, Alan 1117
Walsh, A. 1118

Walsh, J. 1119, 1120
Walton, Ortiz 1121
Ware, H. 307
Ware, Harriett 155, 344
Ware, Helen 76
Ware, William Porter 45
Warfield, Sandra 791
Warner, Mrs. Charles Dudley 173
Warren, Dale 1122
Warren, J. 308
Warren, L. 1123
Warwick, Dionne 497, 703, 774, 991
Waters, Ethel 863, 1124, 1125
Watkins, M. F. 309
Weathers, Felicia 394
Wechsberg, Joseph 310
Weilich, L. 311
Weinstock, Herbert 1126, 1187
Weldon, Constance 648
Weller, Sheila 1127
Wells, Kitty 577
West, Hilda 454
West, Stephen 1128, 1129
White, Jackie 1131
Wiggins, Ella Mae 183
Wilgus, D. K. 1133
Wilkin, Marijohn 380
Wilkinson, G. 1134
Willard, Frances Elizabeth 315
William, Camilla 357
Williams, B. 1135, 1136, 1137, 1138
Williams, Katherine 316
Williams, Martin T. 1139, 1140, 1141, 1142, 1143, 1144
Williams, Mary Lou 534, 963
Williams, Ora 1305
Williams, Paul 1145
Williams, Richard 1146
Willis, Ellen 1147, 1148

Wilmer, Valerie 1149
Wilson, A. 317
Wilson, Mary 829, 1059
Wilson, Nancy 935, 1063, 1140
Wilson, T. 1150
Winsor, Justin 1269
Winstone, E. 1151
Wisneski, Herbert 1152
Wodehouse, P. G. 1153
Womenfolk 1164
Wood, Peggy 323
Wood, V. 324
Woodbury, Al 667
Work, John Wesley 325
Wren, Christopher S. 1171
Wright, G. 1172
Wright, Gladys 674
Wurlitzer, Lee 435
Wurm, Marie 327
Wylie, Evan McLeod 686, 1173
Wynette, Tammy 467

Yaw, Ellen Beach 303, 328

Zanzig, Augustus Delafield
Zeschin, Robert 1271
Ziegfeld Follies 69
Ziegler, Dorothy 648
Zimmermann, G. 1176
Zucca, Manna 286

45364

[S]wronski, JoAnn

[Wo]men in American
[mu]sic, a bibliog-
[ra]phy